PRENTICE-HALL
Foundations of Cultural Geography Series
PHILIP L. WAGNER, *Editor*

RURAL LANDSCAPES OF THE NONWESTERN WORLD,
James M. Blaut

RURAL LANDSCAPES OF THE WESTERN WORLD,
John Fraser Hart

GEOGRAPHY OF DOMESTICATION, *Erich Isaac*

FRONTIERS OF POLITICAL GEOGRAPHY, *Roger E. Kasperson*

CULTURAL ECOLOGY, *Marvin W. Mikesell*

MIGRATION AND DIFFUSION, *Forrest R. Pitts*

HOUSE FORM AND CULTURE, *Amos Rapoport*

GEOGRAPHY OF RELIGIONS, *David E. Sopher*

GEOGRAPHY OF CITIES, *James E. Vance, Jr.*

ENVIRONMENTS AND PEOPLES, *Philip L. Wagner*

CULTURAL GEOGRAPHY OF THE UNITED STATES,
Wilbur Zelinsky

A PROLOGUE TO POPULATION GEOGRAPHY, *Wilbur Zelinsky* *

RICHARD E. DAHLBERG, *Series Cartographer*

* *In Prentice-Hall's Foundations of Economic Geography Series, also.*

Foundations of Cultural Geography Series

RICHARD E. DAHLBERG, *Series Cartographer*

Lj Keeler

House Form
and
Culture

AMOS RAPOPORT
University College London

PRENTICE-HALL, INC., Englewood Cliffs, N.J.

to my parents

Library of Congress Catalog Card No.: 69-14550

Current printing (last number):
10   9   8   7   6   5

Drawings and photographs by the author.

PRENTICE-HALL INTERNATIONAL, INC., *London*
PRENTICE-HALL OF AUSTRALIA, PTY. LTD., *Sydney*
PRENTICE-HALL OF CANADA, LTD., *Toronto*
PRENTICE-HALL OF INDIA PRIVATE LTD., *New Delhi*
PRENTICE-HALL OF JAPAN, INC., *Tokyo*

Foundations of Cultural Geography Series

The title of this series, Foundations of Cultural Geography, represents its purpose well. Our huge and highly variegated store of knowledge about the ways that humans occupy and use their world becomes most meaningful when studied in the light of certain basic questions. Original studies of such basic questions make up this series of books by leading scholars in the field.

The authors of the series report and evaluate current thought centered on the questions: How do widely different systems of ideas and practice influence what people do to recreate and utilize their habitats? How do such systems of thought and habitat spread and evolve? How do human efforts actually change environments, and with what effects?

These questions are approached comparatively, respecting the great range of choice and experience available to mankind. They are treated historically as well, to trace and interpret and assess what man has done at various times and places. They are studied functionally, too, and whatever controlling processes and relationships they may reveal are sought.

Diverse tastes and talents govern the authors' attack on these problems. One deals with religion as a system of ideas both influencing and reflecting environmental conditions. Another evaluates the role of belief and custom in reshaping plant and animal species to human purposes. Some consider the use and meaning of human creations, like houses or cities, in geographic context; others treat of the subtle and complex relationships with nature found in agricultural systems of many sorts. One author looks at an entire country as a culturally-shaped environment; another analyzes the mechanics of the spread of customs and beliefs in space. All work toward an understanding of the same key problems. We invite the reader to participate actively in the critical rethinking by which scholarship moves forward.

PHILIP L. WAGNER

Mankind's dwellings hold a double fascination for the cultural geographer. Not only do they commonly contribute much to the distinctive character of landscapes, they also stand as the concrete expressions of a complex interaction among cultural skills and norms, climatic conditions, and the potentialities of natural materials. Professor Rapoport, a widely traveled architect, considers in this volume how the houses of the world's people thus reflect the physical conditions of their environments, as well as cultural preferences and capabilities, in a wide variety of solutions to basic problems of house design.

PHILIP L. WAGNER

Preface

This book is the result of a number of years' concern with primitive and vernacular buildings and settlements, from the point of view of the environmental designer. The forces that shape these dwellings and give them clearly identifiable characteristics, and their lessons for the present day, have been my primary interests. Some of the ideas presented were explored in a number of courses—the first formally taught on this subject, as far as I know—and the students' enthusiastic acceptance of them has encouraged me to further endeavors, as their criticisms have helped to clarify some of the ideas.

Very little work has been done from the point of view adopted here, and this study must be exploratory. No book on such a vast subject can be final—and this one does not, in fact, represent a generally accepted or shared body of thought. Rather, it is my personal interpretation of the evidence concerning the way in which people organize and use dwelling space. Many of the conclusions will, no doubt, have to be elaborated and revised in the future.

I am not concerned with unique cases or with the multiplicity of examples; there will be no attempt to cover the scattered references or vast related bibliography on specific places and topics. My main interest is in general features, as indeed it must be, given the serious limitations of space which the format imposes and the vastness of the subject, which includes most of what man has built since he began building. With such a vast temporal and spatial distribution, there is an ever-present danger of becoming involved in too much detail.

The book tries to propose a conceptual framework for looking at the great variety of house types and forms and the forces that affect them. It attempts to bring some order to this complex field and thus create a better understanding of the form determinants of dwellings.

This is a subject which overlaps many disciplines—architecture, cultural geography, history, city planning, anthropology, ethnography, cross-cultural studies, and even the behavioral sciences. It is therefore necessarily cross-disciplinary and must call on the work of many observers in diverse fields and reflect many intellectual debts. The area of my concern is new not only because my stress is on the *buildings* and their creation, but also because, in many of the fields mentioned, the topic of dwellings and settlements, while relevant, has been either neglected or treated as secondary. When references to dwellings and settlements occur in the anthropological literature, for example, they are *descriptive* rather than analytical; cultural geography, which has seen the dwelling as important, has either used it as a diagnostic tool or concentrated on morphological classification.

In attempting to deal with the broader aspects of house form, this book is addressed to all those concerned with the habitat of man.

Amos Rapoport

Contents

CHAPTER 1 *the nature and*
definition of the field

Architectural theory and history have traditionally been concerned
with the study of monuments. They have emphasized the work of men
of genius, the unusual, the rare. Although this is only right, it has meant
that we have tended to forget that the work of the designer, let alone
of the designer of genius, has represented a small, often insignificant,
portion of the building activity at any given period. The physical environment of man, especially the built environment, has not been, and
still is not, controlled by the designer. This environment is the result
of vernacular (or folk, or popular) architecture, and it has been largely
ignored in architectural history and theory. Yet it has been the environment of the Athens of the Acropolis, of the Maya cities and the towns
next to Egyptian temples and tombs or around Gothic cathedrals—as it
has been of remote villages and islands, whether of Greece or the South
Seas. In addition, the high style buildings usually must be seen in relation to, and in the context of, the vernacular matrix, and are in fact
incomprehensible outside that context, especially as it existed at the time
they were designed and built.

In archeology, the interest shifted a while ago from temples, palaces,
and tombs to the whole city as an expression of a culture and a way
of life, although the house, the most typically vernacular building type,
is still frequently ignored. Similar shifts have taken place in general history, in the history of art, and in that of music, to an extent. In architecture, however, such an interest is only now starting, and it has not
yet gone very far nor beyond the purely visual. It is therefore a topic
which has been rather neglected.

This neglect of the bulk of the built environment, the tendency to
see mud hovels or insignificant grass shacks where there are, in fact,
buildings of great quality with much to teach us, has given rise to two

standards—one for "important" buildings, especially those of the past, and another for "unimportant" buildings and the environment which they compose. This approach suggests that architecture is to be found only in the monuments and that there is a difference in the way one judges a masterpiece, whether of the past or of today, as compared to the house in which one lives, or in which the peasant lived; the Royal plaza and the street which led to it, or of one's own street. Yet we must look at the whole environment in order to understand it, and it is in this sense that we must study the history of built form. If we look at only the smallest part of the work, that part tends to assume undue importance; if we look at it in isolation, we cannot grasp its complex and subtle relation to the vernacular matrix with which it forms a total spatial and hierarchic system. Neglect of the vernacular buildings which form the environment has had the effect of making the latter seem unimportant; it is consequently neglected physically and constantly deteriorates.

What then do we mean by folk architecture and by the terms *primitive* and *vernacular* as they apply to building forms?

It is possible, first of all, to distinguish between buildings belonging to the grand design tradition and those of the folk tradition.[1]

We may say that monuments—buildings of the grand design tradition—are built to impress either the populace with the power of the patron, or the peer group of designers and cognoscenti with the cleverness of the designer and good taste of the patron. The folk tradition, on the other hand, is the direct and unself-conscious translation into physical form of a culture, its needs and values—as well as the desires, dreams, and passions of a people. It is the world view writ small, the "ideal" environment of a people expressed in buildings and settlements, with no designer, artist, or architect with an axe to grind (although to what extent the designer is really a form *giver* is a moot point). The folk tradition is much more closely related to the culture of the majority and life as it is really lived than is the grand design tradition, which represents the culture of the elite. The folk tradition also represents the bulk of the built environment.[2]

Within this folk tradition we may distinguish between primitive and vernacular buildings, with the latter comprising preindustrial vernacular

---

[1] This basic distinction relates to a number of studies. For example, see Dwight Macdonald, "Masscult and Midcult," in *Against the American Grain* (New York: Random House, Inc., 1962); Robert Redfield, *The Primitive World and its Transformations* (Ithaca, N.Y.: Cornell University Press, 1953), and *Peasant Society and Culture* (Chicago: University of Chicago Press, 1965). In the latter, pp. 70 ff., the distinction is made between the great tradition and the little tradition (high culture and low culture; classic culture and folk culture; the learned and popular tradition; hierarchic and lay culture). This applies to many fields—music, religion, medicine, literature, and others—but has not been applied to architecture to any extent.

[2] Even today the figure for architect-designed buildings worldwide is reliably estimated at five per cent. See Constantinos A. Doxiadis, *Architecture in Transition* (London: Hutchinson, Ltd., 1964), pp. 71-75. The maximum, he estimates, is reached in England where architects may be responsible for 40 per cent of the buildings. In most of the world their influence is "precisely nil" (p. 71), five per cent of all buildings being designed by architects. Most buildings are built by the people or by tradesmen.

and modern vernacular. Present-day design, while part of the grand design tradition, is characterized by a greater degree of institutionalization and specialization.

Primitive is much easier to define than *vernacular*. Neither *vernacular* nor *anonymous* is a very satisfactory term for identifying this form of architecture. The French *architecture populaire* may be the most satisfactory.[3]

Primitive building, most simply, refers to that produced by societies defined as primitive by anthropologists. It refers largely to certain technological as well as economic levels of development, but also includes aspects of social organization.[4] While the dwellings produced in such a culture may, at first glance and by our *technological* standards, appear elementary, they are, in fact, built by people using their intelligence, ability—no different from ours—and resources to their fullest extent. The term *primitive*, therefore, does not refer to the builders' intentions or abilities, but rather to the society in which they build. It is of course a relative term; to future societies we will undoubtedly appear rather primitive.

Redfield points out that in primitive societies there is a diffuse knowledge of everything by all, and every aspect of tribal life is everybody's business.[5] There is no technical vocabulary, because there is little specialization beyond age and sex—although some specialization in religious knowledge is occasionally found. This is, of course, linked to Redfield's definition of primitive as preliterate,[6] and in terms of building this implies that everyone is capable of building his own dwelling—and usually does. Trades are hardly differentiated, and the average family has all the available technical knowledge. Any member of the group can build the buildings which the group needs, although in many cases, for social as well as technical reasons, this is done cooperatively by a larger group.[7]

---

3 The dictionary defines *popular* as being of, pertaining to, or originating from the common people as distinguished from a select portion. *Vernacular* is defined as indigenous, used by the people; *anonymous* as of unknown authorship; *folk* as masses of the people in the lower culture, and originated or widely used among common people. In the latter case the use of *folk culture* in a different sense by Gideon Sjoberg (*The Preindustrial City—Past and Present*, Glencoe, Ill.: The Free Press, 1960) and Redfield (*The Primitive World and Its Transformations*) is a problem. The division into primitive, vernacular, and grand design tradition may, indeed, correspond to Redfield's and Sjoberg's division into three types of societies—folk, peasant or traditional, and civilized. There may also be a possible relation to David Riesman's tradition oriented, inner directed, and outer directed societies (*The Lonely Crowd*, New Haven: Yale University Press, 1950).

4 For a summary of the definition of *primitive*, see J. Gould and W. L. Kolb, eds., *A Dictionary of the Social Sciences* (UNESCO) (New York: The Free Press, 1964).

5 Robert Redfield, *Peasant Society and Culture*, pp. 72-73.

6 Redfield, *The Primitive World and its Transformations*, p. xi.

7 In some primitive societies, such as those of Polynesia, the ordinary dwelling is built by its inhabitants, and the chief's house or communal house by professional carpenters. In Melanesia, houses are built individually while the chiefs' houses and sacred canoe houses are built by the village as a whole and are the concern of the village. In general, however, it has been suggested that primitive societies despise specialized labor and that this, rather than lack of economic initiative, explains the absence of specialization. See Lewis Mumford, *The City in History* (Harcourt, Brace & World, Inc., 1961), p. 102.

Since the average member of the group builds his own house, he understands his needs and requirements perfectly; any problems that arise will affect him personally and be dealt with. There are, of course, prescribed ways of doing and not doing things. Certain forms are taken for granted and strongly resist change, since societies like these tend to be very tradition oriented. This explains the close relation between the forms and the culture in which they are embedded, and also the fact that some of these forms persist for very long periods of time. With this persistence the model is finally adjusted until it satisfies most of the cultural, physical, and maintenance requirements. This model is fully uniform, and in a primitive society all the dwellings are basically identical.

As I have suggested, a satisfactory definition of *vernacular* is more difficult. At the moment, the most successful way of describing it seems to be in terms of process—how it is "designed" and built.

When building tradesmen are used for construction of most dwellings, we may arbitrarily say that primitive building gives way to *preindustrial vernacular*.[8] Even in this case, however, everyone in the society knows the building types and even how to build them, the expertise of the tradesman being a matter of degree. The peasant owner is still very much a *participant* in the design process, not merely a *consumer;* this applies to the townsman of a preindustrial culture to a greater extent than it does to the townsman of today, since participation tends to decrease with urbanization and greater specialization. This change to the use of tradesmen marks the beginning of the process of increasing specialization of trades, although at the outset of this process the tradesman is such only part-time, and is still also a peasant. The two methods of building may, in fact, coexist as they do in the primitive context. In preindustrial vernacular the accepted *form* still exists, thus offering a way of arriving at a definition of vernacular by looking at the "design process."

The vernacular design process is one of models and adjustments or variations, and there is more individual variability and differentiation than in primitive buildings; it is the *individual specimens* that are modified, not the *type*. When a tradesman builds a farmhouse for a peasant, they both know the type in question, the form or model, and even the materials. What remains to be determined are the specifics—family requirements (although this is also less variable than is true today), size (depending on wealth), and relation to the site and micro-climate.[9] Since

---

[8] An alternative way of drawing a distinction between primitive and vernacular is suggested by an analogy with Redfield's *Peasant Society and Culture,* pp. 68-69, 71, where primitive is defined as isolated and self-contained—if not in terms of other primitive cultures then in terms of some *high* culture—while peasant cultures (i.e., vernacular) must be seen in the context of the coexisting high cultures. They are replenished and influenced by the high culture because they are aware of it, and the high and low cultures are interdependent and affect each other. An example would be the influence of the Baroque on the wooden farmhouses of Switzerland and Austria. There is a connection between vernacular and high-style buildings (although causal connections are difficult to establish), while this connection does *not* exist in primitive cultures which have no knowledge of an outside high culture.

[9] See J. A. Bundgaard, *Mnesicles* (Copenhagen: Gyldendal, 1957), in which he suggests that Greek temples are vernacular forms in this sense.

both tradesman and peasant agree on what is wanted, there is, in effect, a model which is adjusted and adapted as one proceeds; this is as true of the Danish farmer as of the French or Yugoslav peasant. The best description I know of this process is found in a Yugoslavian book describing the "design" of a house in Sarajevo during the Islamic period.

One day the owner of the neighbouring garden brought a carpenter to the site and told him to build-up a house. They stopped on a spot where the ground sloped gently downwards. The carpenter had a look at the trees, the ground, the environments, and the town in the valley. Then he proceeded to extract from his cummerbund some pegs, paced off the distances, and marked them with the pegs. [Note that there is no question of *what type* of house is to be built—there is a self-evident accepted model.] Thus he came to his *main* task [italics added]. He asked the owner which trees might be sacrificed, moved his pegs for a few feet, nodded and seemed satisfied. He found that the new house would not obstruct the view from the neighbouring structures . . . [and then he goes on to examine light, sun, water, and so on].[10]

These are, of course, what I have called the adjustments to the model. One starts with the simplest outline, the main features, and adds and elaborates the details and makes adjustments as one proceeds. The outline is in the mind's eye at the start, and even the execution involves the use of principles applicable to every building; the form also adjusts to given problems and available means without *conscious* aesthetic striving or stylistic interests. Such buildings are based on the idea that a common task should be performed in the simplest, most unobtrusive and direct way possible. This can only occur in a society which is tradition bound, where the few changes that occur happen within a frame of a given common heritage and hierarchy of values reflected in the building types.[11]

The Bosnian description sums up the characteristics of vernacular building as I see them: lack of theoretical or aesthetic pretensions; working *with* the site and micro-climate; respect for other people and *their* houses and hence for the total environment, man-made as well as natural; and working within an idiom with variations within a given order. There are many individual variations within a framework which can be adapted in various ways. Although a vernacular always has limitations in the range of expression possible, at the same time it can fit many different situations, and create a *place* at each. It is, of course, precisely this limitation of expression which makes any communication possible. To communicate, one must be prepared to learn as well as use the language—which implies the acceptance of authority, trust, and a shared vocabulary.

Another characteristic of vernacular is its additive quality, its un-

10 D. Grabrijan and J. Neidhardt, *Architecture of Bosnia* (Ljubljana: Državna Založba Slovenije, 1957), p. 313.
11 For example, see the great variety of houses in Japan, all of which are variations on a model in my terms. Bruno Taut shows how owner and designer can immediately agree on what to do, and the owner, in effect, is also the designer. See his *Houses and People of Japan*, 2nd ed. (Tokyo: Sanseido Co., 1958), pp. 27, 31. In Switzerland every valley has a typical form of farmhouse—the model—with many individual variations within that basic type.

specialized, open-ended nature, so different from the closed, final form typical of most high-style design. It is this quality which enables vernacular buildings to accept changes and additions which would visually and conceptually destroy a high-style design. Vernacular is also characterized by the greater importance and significance of relationships between elements, and the manner in which these relationships are achieved, rather than by the nature of the elements themselves. This, however, leads us into the realm of urban design, which is the topic for another book.

The model itself is the result of the collaboration of many people over many generations as well as the collaboration between makers and users of buildings and other artifacts, which is what is meant by the term *traditional*. Since knowledge of the model is shared by all, there is no need for drawings or designers. A house is meant to be like all the well-built houses in a given area. The construction is simple, clear, and easy to grasp, and since everyone knows the rules, the craftsman is called in only because he has a more *detailed* knowledge of these rules. Size, layout, relation to site, and other variables can be decided by discussion and, if necessary, set down in a written contract. The aesthetic quality is not specially created for each house—it is traditional and handed down through the generations. Tradition has the force of a law honored by everyone through collective assent. It is thus accepted and obeyed, since respect for tradition gives collective control, which acts as a discipline. This approach works because there is a shared image of life, an accepted model of buildings, a small number of building types, and, finally, an accepted *hierarchy* and hence an accepted settlement pattern. As long as the tradition is alive, this shared and accepted image operates; when tradition goes, the picture changes. Without tradition, there can no longer be reliance on the accepted norms, and there is a beginning of institutionalization. The introduction of pattern books is the first step in this process, as in the United States with barns and houses and in Japan with houses. Tradition as a regulator has disappeared—notably in our own culture—for a number of reasons.

The first reason is the greater number of building types, many of which are too complex to build in traditional fashion. This rise of specialization and differentiation is paralleled in the spaces within the buildings and the various trades and professions involved in their design and erection.

The second reason is loss of the common shared value system and image of the world, with a consequent loss of an accepted and shared hierarchy—and generally a loss of goals shared by designers and the public. This results in the disappearance of that spirit of cooperation which makes people respect the rights of adjoining people and their buildings, and ultimately the rights of the settlement as a whole. Lack of cooperation leads to the introduction of such controls (going beyond pattern books) as codes, regulations, and zoning rules concerning alignments and setbacks, which also existed in some preindustrial towns. For example, in Latin America under the Spanish, the Laws of the Indies prescribed narrow streets for shade, uniformity of facades, and orientation for winds; while Peking had rules regulating the hierarchy of colors. These rules do not usually work as well as the voluntary controls of public opinion. The distinction between traditional and modern societies can be understood in terms of the contrast between informal controls, affectivity, and consensus in the former, and impersonality and interdependent specialization in the latter,[12] which would seem to correspond to Redfield's concept of substitution of the technical order for the moral order.[13] While these concepts have usually been applied to social mechanisms and cities, they are useful to an understanding of the processes of creating vernacular buildings and settlements.

The third reason for the disappearance of tradition as a regulator is the fact that our culture puts a premium on *originality*, often striving for it for its own sake. As a result, society becomes dissatisfied with traditional forms, and the vernacular process can no longer work. This dissatisfaction is often based on nonfunctional considerations and is linked to socio-cultural factors. In most traditional cultures, novelty is not only not sought after, but is regarded as undesirable.

This book is concerned only in passing with modern vernacular and the question as to whether, in fact, it exists at all. Neither is it really concerned with architect designed buildings. However, some reference needs to be made to these in order to complete the definition of vernacular and to clarify the areas of our concern. Avoiding for the moment the problem of whether a vernacular architecture is possible with modern communications and self-consciousness, I would suggest that there *is* a modern folk idiom, and that this is primarily, although not exclusively, one of *type*. Most of the folk architecture in contemporary America has been in terms of new types—the motel, the diner, drive-ins of all types—all of which originated outside the design professions and have, as it were, come up from "below." The forms themselves have been those currently fashionable and commonly used; their wide dissemination by the various news media, films, and travel make it impossible to create forms in the traditional manner. I have already suggested that relationships between these buildings can no longer be achieved through the informal controls typical of traditional vernacular. Those forms which are still partly of that style—the Doggie Diners, concrete doughnuts, and so on—are designed *for* the popular taste, not *by* it, but they, as well as popular housing, continue to show some commonly held values more clearly than does the design subculture.

Finally we find that due to the causes already enumerated—greater complexity of problems and greater specialization—the design of buildings and settlements is increasingly the concern of professional designers.

[12] Gerald Breese, *Urbanization in Newly Developing Countries* (Englewood Cliffs, N.J.: Prentice-Hall, Inc., 1966), p. 7. See also Eric Wolf, *Peasants* (Englewood Cliffs, N.J.: Prentice-Hall, Inc., 1966), p. 11, in which he similarly distinguishes between primitive and "civilized" in terms of specialization and differentiation.

[13] Redfield, *The Primitive World and Its Transformations,* and Redfield and Singer, "The Cultural Role of Cities," *Economic Development and Cultural Change,* 3 (October 1954), esp. pp. 56-57.

What we find, in effect, is a double change in the way built form is produced:

1. *Primitive.* Very few building types, a model with few individual variations, *built by all.*

2. *Preindustrial vernacular.* A greater, though still limited, number of building types, more individual variation of the model, *built by tradesmen.*

3. *High-style and modern.* Many specialized building types, each building being an original creation (although this may be changing), *designed and built by teams of specialists.*

These changes clearly involve a process of differentiation in building types and spaces, the building process, and the trades involved.

This development is also found in other fields, such as textiles, tools, and pottery. In the case of the latter, for example, development starts with the individual family making its own pots, then continues with the craftsman potter, and finally evolves to the artist potter or the specialist designers of mass-produced pottery. It is in these terms of a process of differentiation that changes from primitive to vernacular and then to industrial vernacular and modern can best be understood.

Differentiation and the Nature of the Evidence

Lack of differentiation in the forms and construction of buildings is an expression of the general lack of differentiation typical of primitive and even peasant societies. This aspect of these societies affects the types of buildings and hence the type of evidence which we need to consider.

Almost all observers of primitive and peasant societies have commented on the typical lack of differentiation in the use of space and labor which also permeates other areas of life and thought.[14] There is no separation among man's life, work, and religion, and very little differentiation, if any, between the sacred and the profane. Religion is so closely linked as to be inseparable from social life and needs. Jung has commented on the lack of sharp boundaries between man and animals in the primitive world,[15] and Giedion also comments on this, stressing the general lack of differentiation between man and nature, and between directions in cave art; he equates the rise of the first high civilizations with man becoming more important than animals, and with the rise of the vertical as a preferred direction.[16] Giedion's hypothesis is supported

---

[14] See, for example, Robert Redfield, *A Village That Chose Progress: Chan Kom Revisited* (Chicago: University of Chicago Press, 1950), pp. 25, 61, where he compares Chan Kom with the way it had been before. One could sum up the changes under increasing differentiation, both at the scale of the village as a whole, with the breaking up into neighborhoods, and in terms of public and private space—the plaza and patio. The latter could be equated with Dan Stanislawski's comparison of Indian and Spanish towns in Michoacan, *The Anatomy of Eleven Towns in Michoacan,* University of Texas, Institute of Latin American Studies (Austin: University of Texas Press, 1950).

[15] Carl Jung, *Man and His Symbols* (Garden City, N.Y.: Doubleday and Co., 1964), p. 45.

[16] Siegfried Giedion, *The Eternal Present,* vols. 1 and 2, Bollingen XXXV (New York: Pantheon Books, 1964).

by the evidence of some present day "stone-age" civilizations, such as the Eskimos, who show this lack of differentiation conceptually and in the lack of preferred directions in art, confirming the late emergence of such directions as the vertical.[17] Max Sorre's concept of the *Genre de vie* embraces as many spiritual elements as material and social ones because of this unity and lack of differentiation between magic and work, religious and secular. This applies to work in general, which is undifferentiated or, as we would say, unspecialized, and hence applies to the way in which space is used. As spaces become more separated and differentiated, the number of types of spaces increases. For example, from man and animals being housed in the same room, as in the Kabylie, we find them under one roof but in separate spaces, as in Switzerland, then separated but close, as in the French farmhouse, and finally widely separated. The same applies to differentiation of spaces within the house for various uses.

Compare, for instance, the Japanese farmhouse, where living, stabling of horses, and rearing of silkworms take place in the same space, or the village or town house where the same applies to living, shop, and workshop, as well as lack of differentiation of rooms in the house, with our own use of spaces and separation of work and living.

The medieval house shows the rise of differentiation in three respects. At first work and living become somewhat differentiated with separate shop and house entrances; then the sleeping quarters for apprentices and workers, on the first floor, become separated from family sleeping and living, which take place in a large room on the second floor; finally, a separation of living from sleeping rooms takes place in the family quarters.[18]

Even a house plan as complex and highly differentiated as the Moslem house of Turkey and Yugoslavia has different uses for rooms at different times of the day,[19] and peasant cultures still show a combination of home and economic unit in one place. With increase in the complexity of civilization comes ever greater differentiation of types of building and urban space, and separation of uses culminating in the extreme zoning practices of today.

This multiple use of space greatly affects the form of the house and settlement, and means that the evidence which we need to consider in this book comprises very few building types. Since the house is little differentiated internally and most activities take place in it, or in its immediate setting, the only other buildings in primitive cultures are a few shrines, chiefs' houses, granaries—often linked with the house—and storehouses, which may be sacred. Even in preindustrial cultures the

---

[17] E. Carpenter, "Image Making in Arctic Art," in *Sign, Image, Symbol*, ed. G. Kepes (New York: George Braziller, Inc., 1966), pp. 206 ff. (See especially pp. 212, 214-216, 218-219.)

[18] Gianni Pironne, *Une Tradition Européenne dans L'Habitation*, "Aspects Européens" Council of Europe Series A (Humanities), No. 6 (Leiden: A. W. Sythoff, 1963), pp. 17, 37-38.

[19] Grabrijan and Neidhardt, *Architecture of Bosnia*, pp. 171, 238, 289, and elsewhere.

vast mass of vernacular buildings, urban and rural, consists of dwellings in this undifferentiated sense. The concentration on houses in this study is also due to the fact that they show most clearly the link between form and life patterns, and very few non-houses can be considered as vernacular forms, although some religious buildings fall into this category,[20] as do some workshops, mills, and other buildings which now form the new field of industrial archeology. Most of these nondomestic forms tend to be more design oriented and more affected by the high culture coexistent with them in preindustrial and peasant cultures than are the houses. Finally, houses also provide the best way of relating the whole system of house, settlement, landscape, and monumental buildings to the way of life.

Almost every culture, with a few exceptions, has buildings of religious or social significance, often both at the same time, which possess greater symbolic value and content than the ordinary dwellings.[21] This is generally shown by their greater scale, more elaborate decoration, and method of building, but they may also be distinguished by being smaller; [22] in any case, they are *different*. These are the monumental buildings of a culture which tend to stand for more than the house—which, as I will try to show, also stands for more than is generally assumed.

The distinction becomes clear if one compares the "sleeping bag" of the Sepik River area of New Guinea, a series of hoops just big enough for one person to slide into, with the decorated meeting house 60 feet high and up to 135 feet long (the *Tambaran*), which is also the men's dwelling and cult place, forbidden to women. This contrast of huge meeting houses and small dwellings is typical of this area in general, and will be discussed later in more detail. In the Solomons and Melanesia the chiefs' houses and canoe houses, all the public buildings, in fact, are more elaborate than the dwellings, while in Tahiti temples are built of stone whereas houses are always of wood. The temple in an Indian town, or the church or cathedral in Europe or the United States, is also very different from the surrounding houses.

Any emotional or religious surplus, and therefore *material* surplus, which is extremely limited in societies of scarcity, is reserved for these special types of buildings, and then there is always a hierarchy present. The surplus is reserved for monuments of the culture—the shrine, clan house, chief's house, or container of ritual objects. In building houses, therefore, primitive people generally work right up to the technological ceiling of their culture, but well below the aesthetic ceiling demonstrated by these other buildings, as well as by weapons, costumes, and other

[20] Amos Rapoport, "Sacred Space in Primitive and Vernacular Architecture," *Liturgical Arts*, XXXVI, No. 2 (February 1968), 36-40.

[21] Pierre Deffontaines, *Géographie et Religions*, 9th ed. (Paris: Gallimard, 1948), pp. 69-70, names some cultures that have no cult buildings and use trees, stones, and so on, as sacred places. They may, of course, still have chiefs' houses and other buildings of this type.

[22] For example, see Alain Gheerbrant, *Journey to the Far Amazon* (New York: Simon & Schuster, 1954), p. 92—the Piaroa Indians' shrine is only 10 feet across, while the house is 50 feet long and 25 feet high.

artifacts.[23] This does not, however, apply universally; the elaborately decorated houses of Africa are one clear exception.

One qualification needs to be made. Many societies display some differentiation in house form based on stratification in that society, whether by military prowess, wealth, or age. In parts of Africa the compound may be larger and have more retainers, wives, or cattle; the house may be more decorated, as in Southeast Asia; the roof may have more bands of thatching, as among the Peul of Africa. The skulls or scalps of enemies may be displayed as symbols, or the wealth and prestige of the owner may be expressed through size and number of retainers or elaboration of the carved columns, as among the Kwakiutl. The frequent concentration of such decoration on supports and doors, often the most decorated part of the house, as in Nigeria, Mongolia, and elsewhere, may be symbolic; such symbolism will become clear later. In most of these primitive and preindustrial cultures, however, differentiation is of degree only, and the basic house type is unchanged—unlike the variety of today or in the eighteenth and nineteenth centuries.

Reasons for Study

In general terms, we are dealing with an aspect of the history of the built environment—if we take history to mean concern with evidence of the past. Human geography has always been linked with history, and even prehistory, and in the past history has also played an important role in architectural studies. Since architectural history has been rather neglected during the last few decades, particularly in the United States, we may ask why architectural history should be studied at this moment in time, with its stress on rapid change.

The assumption behind any historical approach is that one can learn from the past; that study of the past is of value philosophically as well as in making us aware of the complexity and overlapping of things. It can also clarify those elements that are constant and those which change. "We need the rich time dimension to help us avoid the all too common triviality of living in the moment, as a continuous prelude to rushing thoughtlessly into the future." [24] Hence we cannot assume a sudden break with all that went before, or that we and our problems are so different that the past has no lessons for us. While technology may progress, architecture does not necessarily do so.

Buildings, as all human endeavors, obey varied and often contradictory and conflicting impulses which interefere with the simple and orderly diagrams, models, and classifications we love to construct. The complexities of man and his history cannot be encompassed in neat formulas, although the desire to do so characterizes our age. Rather than eliminate these contradictions, in accordance with what could be called

[23] A. H. Brodrick, "Grass Roots," *Architectural Review* (London), CXV, No. 686 (February 1954), 101-111.
[24] G. Evelyn Hutchinson in S. Dillon Ripley, ed., *Knowledge Among Men*, Smithsonian Institution Symposium (New York: Simon and Schuster, 1966), p. 85.

the *Procrustes' bed syndrome*, it would seem that the simple models should be revised so as to preserve the sense of the contradictions and complexities of the relations among dwellings, settlements, culture, and the continuity of man's achievement.

With regard to the specific topic as I have defined it, the question still arises—why study primitive and preindustrial house form in the space age, with its rapid tempo of change? One reason is that these houses, being the *direct* expression of changing values, images, perceptions, and ways of life, as well as of certain constancies, become a very fruitful topic for study. Another important aspect in this connection is the need for cross-cultural studies and comparisons, which are useful in two ways. First, from the practical point of view, different cultures and subcultures coexist in our cities, with the consequent need for different housing and settlement patterns; this applies with even more force to the developing countries (see Chapter 6). Second, and more generally, comparisons of this type can offer an insight into the basic nature of shelter and "dwelling," of the design process and the meaning of "basic needs."

But this need for cross-cultural comparison goes further. In order to understand culture and its relation to housing form, we need the "intellectual encounter with man in all his varieties, no matter how primitive, how ancient, or seemingly insignificant." [25] The value of this kind of study is that it provides a great range of variables in different cultures, as well as greater extremes—hence a greater sense of the range of alternatives possible.

Ruth Benedict has pointed out that all cultures make a selection of their cultural institutions, and that "each from the point of view of another ignores fundamentals and exploits irrelevancies." She refers to such aspects of society as monetary value, which may be ignored or of the essence, and technology, which may be strong or "unbelievably slighted even in those aspects of life which seem necessary to ensure survival." Some cultures may stress adolescence, others death, and yet others afterlife.[26]

Similar choices apply to the house and the objectives inherent in its design, and for this reason we need to look at other cultures, distant both in space and time. Such an examination would show, for example, that novelty, which has been considered a major characteristic of architecture, is in fact *atypical* of most primitive and vernacular buildings, and is a culturally linked phenomenon of recent vintage. This can be understood only through comparison with the earlier vernacular, a comparison necessary in order to avoid a distorted view.

In the same way that we cannot understand our subject at a moment in time, we cannot understand it in the context of a single culture. Through seeing other ways of doing things, we are made aware that there

---

[25] E. R. Service, *The Hunters* (Englewood Cliffs, N.J.: Prentice-Hall, Inc., 1966), p. v.

[26] Ruth Benedict, *Patterns of Culture* (Boston: Houghton Mifflin Company, 1959), p. 24.

are other ways, that our way may be peculiar rather than inevitable, and that our values are neither the only ones, nor the norm. Seeing other methods helps us to discover the distinctiveness of our own. Comparisons of this type also make us aware of the problem of constancy and change. It is this aspect of comparative studies that offers the greatest potential from the point of view of architectural—or environmental—theory. The evidence, if considered together with recent work in ethology, ecology, and so on, may well lead to an understanding of the social and psychological aspects of the environment.

The scale at which comparisons are made is of crucial importance. For example, it has been said that modern cultures are hardly different from one another.[27] However, if we look at the scale of the house or room and how it is used, we find significant differences between apparently similar modern industrial cultures.[28] For our purposes, then, we need to look at the micro-scale; generalizations based on too crude a scale may be incorrect or misleading (as will be seen later with regard to building materials). Nevertheless, it is true that modern cultures are more similar, thus providing a good reason for examining primitive and preindustrial cultures. These will show other methods of doing things, other ways of seeing the world, other value systems—and the resulting differing housing and settlement forms. In addition, the recurrence of certain constancies in widely different cultures may take on great significance.

I have already referred to the value for study of the directness with which primitive and preindustrial buildings express the needs and desires of people and the requirements of the cultural and physical milieu without the interference of artistically self-conscious designers. If we regard buildings as the result of the interaction of:

Man—his nature, aspirations, social organization, world view, way of life, social
    and psychological needs, individual and group needs, economic resources,
    attitudes to nature, personality, fashions
    —his physical needs, i.e., the "functional" program
    —the techniques available
Nature—physical aspects, such as climate, site, materials, structural laws, and
    so on
    —visual, such as the landscape

then the influence of man, particularly his personality, both in primitive and vernacular building is less than we commonly find in our culture, and such influences as do exist are not individual or personal, but of the group—and limited at that. Building of this type tends toward a state of balance with nature rather than dominating it, which further reinforces its superiority over the grand design tradition as a topic of study for the relation of the built environment to man and nature.

---

[27] See, for example, Max Sorre in *Readings in Cultural Geography,* Philip L. Wagner and M. W. Mikesell, eds. (Chicago: University of Chicago Press, 1962), p. 370.
[28] See E. T. Hall, *The Silent Language* (Greenwich, Conn.: Fawcett, Premier paperback, 1961), and especially *The Hidden Dimension* (Garden City, N.Y.: Doubleday & Co., 1966).

Finally, because the physical constraints in primitive and preindustrial vernacular buildings are very strong, and the situations tend to be extreme, we are able to examine the influence of different variables on the creation of form more clearly than we could in the contemporary situation or the grand design tradition, where there are fewer constraints (very few in our context) and the situation tends to be vague and fuzzy. We are better able to judge the relative importance of physical and cultural forces as form determinants. Even modern vernacular can tell us things we would miss by looking only at the grand design tradition, as I will try to show in Chapter 6.

Method of Study

If the definition and description given earlier are accepted, then the time during which primitive and vernacular building has gone on depends on level of technology and way of life, rather than on chronology. As long as there are societies which can be regarded as primitive or preindustrial, we would expect to find the corresponding buildings; such societies extend from the dim past to the present day. The traditional nature of such building implies lack of change as one of its principal characteristics. Many examples of present day primitive and vernacular buildings could be cited. Grass huts like those known in the Neolithic age are still used in Fiji, New Guinea, South America, and elsewhere. European Neolithic lake dwellings on stilts seem identical to some in New Guinea, South America, and even some I saw right outside of Singapore. Courtyard houses generally seem to have changed very little, and those used today resemble some of the earliest houses found in Jericho, Çatal Hüyük, or Ur. In fact, the streets of Ur are like those of many towns in the Middle East today. The huts of the Toda in Central India look like those drawn in the *Font de Gaume* caves in Southwest France, while mud brick houses excavated in Hacilar, Turkey, and dating back to 5200 B.C. are like some I saw recently in Iran. The Trulli of Italy and the beehive huts of Africa and Peru resemble early beehive huts in Cyprus; Maya houses in Yucatán today seem identical to those illustrated in contemporary manuscripts, while those in Peru seem identical to the pre-Columbian equivalents (as at Macchu Picchu). In all of these examples, the existence of an accepted model with few major innovations has resulted in the very strong persistence of form.[29]

Primitive and vernacular buildings have coexisted in the same area with both high civilizations and, at the present time, modern technology. While the pyramids, temples, and palaces of Egypt, palaces of Iran, and the temples of Greece were being built, the majority of people were living in vernacular houses; they still do under the vapor trails of jets and the orbits of rockets. Primitive and peasant societies have not questioned the traditional although this is now changing.

[29] Other artifacts, of course, also show this persistence of form. Carts used today in Sind are like those in Mohenjo Daro 4,500 years ago. The reed boats used in the Rhône valley in the nineteenth century were like those of 7500 B.C.

The geographic distribution of these buildings depends on their corresponding cultures. Primitive and vernacular building has existed, at one time or another, everywhere that man has lived. The differences between the types of buildings in different areas are evidence of differences in culture, rituals, ways of life, and social organization, climates and landscapes, and materials and technology available, while the similarities are evidence not only of areas where some or all of these factors have coincided, but also of some basic constancies in man's needs and desires.

Buildings can be studied in different ways. One can look at them chronologically, tracing the development over time either of techniques, forms, and ideas, or of the thoughts of the designer, or one can study them from a specific point of view. In our case the latter is the most useful method, since, as we have seen, primitive and vernacular buildings are distinguished by lack of change, differing in this respect from the more "normal" historical material.[30] These buildings are, therefore, basically nonchronological in nature.[31] In fact, originality and innovation in primitive and vernacular buildings are frowned upon and often condemned. "Customary ways are sacred and it is not uncommon for individuals to be punished for seemingly slight deviations in methods of production." [32] Such buildings are also anonymous, in the sense that they have no known designer and little is known of the name of the owner or the specific circumstances of their erection, since they are the product of the group rather than the individual.

This means that the intellectual development of the designer cannot be used as a method of study either. The evidence of letters, diaries, and architectural theories as evidenced in journals, books, and drawings, which is of such importance in traditional architectural history, is lacking. In view of the great uniformity in space and time of primitive and vernacular buildings, our topic is best approached from a specific point of view analyzing the buildings themselves rather than trying to trace their development.[33]

---

[30] Mircea Eliade and others have pointed out that, for primitive man and even for peasants, time has no lasting influence. Primitive man lives in a continual present and his time conception is *cyclic* rather than linear. See Mircea Eliade, *Cosmos and History—The Myth of the Eternal Return* (New York: Harper Torchbooks, 1959), pp. 4, 90. Peter Collins, in *Changing Ideals in Modern Architecture* (London: Faber & Faber Ltd., 1965), Chap. 2, pp. 29 ff., also points out that the sense of history and development came rather late.

[31] In some cases, of course, it is possible to date vernacular buildings. For example, see Richard Weiss, *Die Häuser und Landschaften der Schweiz* (Erlenbach-Zurich: Eugen Rentsch Verlag, 1959), in which houses are often dated, and one can also trace the impact of the Baroque on farmhouses. Houses can also be dated by comparison with the monuments of known cultures (e.g., the Egyptian houses of a given dynasty). See also G. H. Rivière, *Techniques et architecture* (Paris: Albin Michel, 1945), in which he traces the evolution of the French farmhouse chronologically. Often, however, the year of building is discovered because of the habit of carving dates, not through any stylistic change.

[32] Lord Raglan, *The Temple and the House* (New York: Norton, 1964), p. 196.

[33] It can also be studied by taking a specific *place* and trying to understand the forms of dwellings and settlements in the light of history, location, social aspects, climate, materials, construction techniques, and other variables.

15

It is implicitly accepted that there is a link between behavior and form in two senses: first, in the sense that an understanding of behavior patterns, including desires, motivations, and feelings, is essential to the understanding of built form, since built form is the physical embodiment of these patterns; and second, in the sense that forms, once built, affect behavior and the way of life. Each of these two aspects forms a vast topic in itself, and both are of great interest to the architect and all those concerned with man's habitat. The question, in effect, is concerned with how changes in culture, expressed in behavior, relate to changes in the environment, as shown by physical form. In this book, the first link between behavior and form is of greater interest, and will be discussed in relation to its specific aspects in various places.

This specific method of dealing with the topic brings up the question of how much one can tell from an examination of buildings, or artifacts in general, when no written records exist, and when there may not even be a detailed knowledge of the way of life, the only evidence being the object, building, or settlement itself. While objects can tell us a great deal about a culture,[34] there are three possible cautions to be borne in mind:

1. What have been called "archeologists' screens"—the way in which wrong evidence, one's own attitudes, values, and experiences may be read into the evidence.[35]
2. The fact that some cultures, although they have a very rich and complex life, have almost no artifacts other than their impact on the landscape.[36] While this is rare, it does exist, and there are also areas where material objects may rapidly deteriorate and disappear, or be destroyed.
3. The idea that architecture may be outside a given culture.[37]

The Specific Task

The goal of most of the work which has been done on the topic of primitive and vernacular buildings has been the classification, listing,

---

[34] For example, see Lewis Mumford, *Art and Technics* (New York: Columbia University Press, 1952), p. 20, wherein he analyzes three nudes—by Cranach, Rubens, and Manet—as indicators of three different cultures, philosophies, and ways of looking at the world, and points out that the physical artifacts—the art objects—give the maximum of meaning with the minimum of concrete material.

[35] See particularly Horace Miner, "Body Ritual among the Necirema," *American Anthropologist*, LVIII (1956), 505-7.

[36] See Redfield, *The Primitive World and Its Transformations*, p. 16, referring to the Pitjandjara, an Australian Aboriginal tribe. Note also the Waika Indians of Northern Brazil, who have no clothing and have not yet discovered pots, but have a very rich and complex religious life very different from their low material culture. See also Amos Rapoport, "Yagua, or the Amazon Dwelling," *Landscape*, XVI, 3 (Spring 1967), 27-30, where it is clear that it would be difficult, if not impossible, to discover from the *physical* evidence alone how the problem of privacy is solved.

[37] This idea, suggested by George Kubler in *The Art and Architecture of Ancient America* (Harmondsworth, Middlesex: Penguin Books, 1962), p. 9, and in a more extreme form by N. F. Carver, *Silent Cities* (Tokyo: Shikokushu, 1966), does not hold even for high-style design, and certainly not for primitive and vernacular buildings, which are completely embedded in their culture.

and description of house types and their features. Little attempt has been made to link these forms to life patterns, beliefs, and desires, although form is difficult to understand outside the context of its setting, culture, and the way of life it shelters. When this link has been discussed, it has been in general rather than specific terms, with no attempt made to discover which of the forces acting on house form could be regarded as primary and which could be regarded as secondary or modifying.

These classifications, and descriptions in travel books and elsewhere, all provide sources of material for study, but little insight into how and why form is created. There have also been no attempts to discuss these conflicting theories of house form that have been proposed. *The object of this book is to concentrate on all these aspects.*

This means that I will avoid the listing and classification of the vast mass of material, and will rather try to gain an understanding of how form occurs. The book will try to discover which theoretical statements give the greatest insight into the house and its form, and which examples can most usefully be generalized without necessarily trying to construct a general, universally valid theory. Such an attempt presents particular problems in this case. First, there is no generally accepted conceptual framework, and second, the amount of material is vast and not recorded in any uniform way. It is also not of uniform quality and does not deal with the same aspects, and therefore cannot easily be directly compared.

The specific task, then, becomes to select those features of the house which seem most universal, and to examine them in different contexts so that we can best understand what it is that affects the forms taken by dwellings and groups of dwellings, and also what it is that so easily enables us to tell, often at a glance, the area, culture, or even subculture to which a dwelling or settlement belongs. Instead of trying to describe or classify differences in house forms, their materials, and parts, I will ask *to what these differences can be attributed,* and will try to relate them to the way of life, the image of the good life, social organization, concepts of territoriality, way of handling "basic needs," the link between the dwelling and the settlement pattern, and so forth.

Furthermore, one must be careful not to speak of forces *determining* form. We must speak of coincidences rather than causal "relations," since the complexity of forces precludes our being able to attribute form to given forces or variables.

We need to become aware of the complexity of interactions and the over-all character of the setting, as well as to understand some of the facts and the significance of the material. It is clear that the topic can only be discussed in general terms, not only because of space limitations, but also because the number of examples and forms is too great, as is their spatial and temporal distribution. One can only suggest some of the ways of looking at these forms, in order to give the feel and the sense of the subject—and to awaken interest in it, and sensitivity to it.

CHAPTER **2** *alternative theories*
of house form

The listing and classification of house types and forms have not
given much insight into the processes or determinants of the creation
of form. There have been some attempts to take a deeper and more
theoretical look at the forces that create house form, but most have been
implicit rather than explicit. I will try to state them in clearer terms.
Those theories to be examined are not meant to represent an exhaustive
list; the discussion will be confined to the principal types of explanations,
including physical ones—involving climate and the need for shelter, materials and technology, and site—and social ones—relating to economics,
defense, and religion.

All these attempts have suffered from two faults. First, they have
tended to be largely physical determinist in nature. Second, no matter
which specific form-determinant has been stressed, the theories have
inclined toward a rather excessively simplistic attempt to attribute form
to a *single* cause. They have thus failed to express that complexity which
can be found only through consideration of as many as possible variables
and their effects.

These theories ignore the fact that building form manifests the complex interaction of many factors, and that selection of a single factor,
and changes in the types of factors selected at different periods, are in
themselves social phenomena of great interest. Each of the theories
examined will also be found to fail to account for some obvious and
significant aspects of the problem.

Climate and the Need for Shelter

Climatic determinism has been widely accepted in architecture as
well as in cultural geography, although in the latter it has recently found
rather less favor. One need not deny the importance of climate to ques-

tion its determining role in the creation of built form. Examination of the extreme differences in urban pattern and house types within one area, such as Old and New Delhi, the old and new parts of Fez or Marrakesh, or certain Latin American cities, shows them to be much more related to culture than to climate, and makes any extreme determinist view rather doubtful.

In architecture the climatic determinist view, still rather commonly held, states that primitive man is concerned primarily with shelter, and consequently the imperatives of climate determine form.

We build houses to keep in a consistent climate, and to keep out predators. We grow, gather and eat food to keep our metabolism on an even keel.[1]

While this is questionable in regard to either housing or food today, it is not true even for primitive man, who has many dwelling and food taboos and restrictions within his economies of scarcity. Nonutilitarian factors seem of primary importance even in the critical field of domestication of animals and plants, as will be discussed later in more detail.

With more specific regard to the house, it has been stated that:

Shelter is of supreme importance to man. It is the prime factor in his constant struggle for survival. In his efforts to shelter himself against the extremes of weather and climate he has, over the ages, evolved many types of dwellings, one of which is the court house.[2]

The question is, of course, why the same area has developed both the court house and other forms—as is the case in Greece, where both the Court form and Megaron form were found, or Latin America, where the court house seems more closely related to cultural factors than to climate as a comparison of Indian and Spanish types shows.

A more important consideration is why so many forms of the house have been developed within the limited number of climatic zones. Even the variation among micro-climatic types is relatively smaller than the number of house types frequently found in areas of similar climate, as, for example, in the South Seas. In the latter case, where climate is non-critical, we find a great variety of house types: artificial man-made islands on the barrier reefs of parts of the Solomons and Fiji, pile dwellings in New Guinea, and houses on mountain terraces in the New Hebrides and Espíritu Santo, not to mention the many variations within each type in each area.

While it would be impossible to deny the great importance of shelter

---

[1] L. Bruce Archer, *Systematic Methods for Designers*, reprinted from articles in *Design* (Great Britain) during 1963-1964 (Nos. 172, 174, 176, 181, 188) with revisions, Part 2, p. 2. See also Barr Ferree, "Primitive Architecture," *The American Naturalist*, XXIII, No. 265 (January 1889), 24-32, wherein on p. 24 it is stated, "Food and shelter constitute the first and chief wants of primitive man and to their satisfaction he devotes his dormant energies," and on p. 28, "Cold climates produce communal living," and so on.

[2] N. Schoenauer and S. Seeman, *The Court Garden House* (Montreal: McGill University Press, 1962), p. 3. See also Eglo Benincasa, *L'Arte di habitare nel Mezzogiorno* (Rome: 1955), which also takes a climatic determinist view and says that the court house is a southern form while the hearth belongs to the North.

as an aspect of the house and as a human need, the basic necessity for shelter itself has been questioned. It has been suggested that house building is *not* a natural act and is not universal, since South East Asia, South America, and Australia contain a number of tribes without houses. A most telling example are the Ona of Tierra del Fuego. Although the climate there is almost arctic, and the ability to build well is shown by the presence of elaborate conical huts for ritual purposes, only wind-breaks are used as dwellings.[3] In Tasmania the aborigines also had no houses in an area of cold climate, but their ability to build was not developed beyond the windbreak.

Conversely, elaborate dwellings are found in areas where, *in terms of climate alone*, the need for shelter is minimal, as in parts of the South Seas. Furthermore, a number of activities in which protection from the weather would seem to be particularly critical, such as cooking, childbirth, and dying, take place in some areas either in the open or in a lean-to.[4] The principle that religious proscriptions and taboos introduce *discomfort* and complications, and become more important than climatic imperatives, is more significant than any specific examples which could be given.

In severe climates, such as the Arctic, the forms of the dwellings of different peoples may be very different—as are those of the Eskimo and the Athabascans—and these forms cannot be explained in terms of climate alone. For example, the Eskimo summer and winter dwellings (the tent and the igloo) have a similar plan consisting of a central space with rooms arranged radially off it. This plan is not found in other cultures in similar climates, and is not the most efficient climatically.[5] If the arctic dwelling is not determined by climate it becomes difficult to accept the suggestion that the round house typical of the Loyalty islands and New Caledonia, and also found in the highland valleys of New Guinea and New Britain, is used because it retains the heat of quite a small fire all night without the need for coverings.[6]

There are cases in which the way of life may lead to almost anti-climatic solutions, with the dwelling form related to economic activity rather than climate. For example, the Hidatsa of the Missouri valley were agriculturalists from April to November, growing corn, greens, and beans.

---

[3] J. H. Steward, ed., *Handbook of South American Indians,* Vol. 1 (Washington: U. S. Government Printing Office, 1964), pp. 110, 120, 137.

[4] Lord Raglan, *The Temple and the House* (New York: W. W. Norton & Company, Inc., 1964), Chaps. 5-8, pp. 42 ff. See also *Aspects de la Maison dans le Monde* (Brussels: Centre International d'étude Ethnographique de la Maison dans le Monde), p. 14.

[5] Edmund Carpenter, "Image Making in Arctic Art," in *Sign, Image, Symbol*, ed. Gyorgy Kepes, pp. 206 ff. See especially p. 221: "Eskimos with a magnificent disregard for environmental determinism open up rather than enclose space. They must, of course, create sealed-off areas, but instead of resorting to boxes, they build complex many-roomed igloos which have as many dimensions and as much freedom as a cloud." (New York: George Braziller, copyright © 1966. Reprinted with the permission of the publisher.)

[6] Jean Guiart, *Arts of the South Pacific,* trans. A. Christie (New York: Golden Press, 1963), p. 10.

During that period they lived in circular wooden houses 30 to 40 feet in diameter, with five-foot-high walls made of tree trunks and four central columns 14 feet high supporting rafters carrying branches, earth, and grass roofing. These houses were in large villages and lasted several generations. From December to March they hunted buffalo and used tepees like those of the plains Indians. The two dwelling types were thus adapted to the two ways of life and the dual economic base, although climatically the reverse would be expected (as is found in Siberia). In other areas of the Missouri valley, where the climate was identical, but the Indians' economy was based entirely on hunting, tepees were the only house form used. Among the Southwest Pomo (Kashaya) Indians of California the *location* of villages changed, being on the coast in summer and on the ridges of the hills in winter, but the form of the house did not change. The main effect of climatic influence was that the house door faced away from the wind.

The existence of fairly frequent anticlimatic solutions leads one to question the more extreme climatic determinist views, and suggests that other forces must be at work. Primitive and peasant builders have needs and drives which are "irrational" in terms of climate. These may include ceremonial and religious beliefs, prestige, status, and so on.

The Boro of the Western Amazon, and a number of other tribes in the Amazon area, live in large communal houses with thickly thatched roofs and walls. There is no provision at all for cross-ventilation, an essential in the hot, humid climate. It would be difficult to find a worse solution in terms of climatic comfort, although it may be good protection against insects. One assumption might be that these houses were introduced from elsewhere, and are the status symbol of some more powerful group. The typical open house used in the jungle area around Iquitos [7] can be seen in the native port of Belén in Iquitos with the identical frame and construction, the addition of *solid walls* being the only major change. This makes the house much more uncomfortable, but may be due to the desire for status in the new culture, and almost certainly reflects new attitudes to, and requirements of, *privacy* (see figs. 2.1 and 2.2).

Anticlimatic solutions can be found in many parts of the world. In the Amazon, wise jungle settlers got Indians to build houses for them, but the Rubber Barons imported brick and marble and built thick-walled mansions. These absorbed and held the moisture, mouldered, and led to disease. They still stand, deserted and ruined, lived in only by squatters who cannot afford anything better.[8]

A similar cultural import is the Chinese house in Malaya, which came from a very different area yet is built side by side with the Malay house, which is much better suited to the climate. The former, of course, is urban and the latter rural, but the courtyard plan and heavy masonry construction of the Chinese house make little sense in the hot, humid area.

[7] Amos Rapoport, "Yagua, or the Amazon Dwelling," *Landscape*, XVI, No. 3 (Spring 1967), 27-30.
[8] Willard Price, *The Amazing Amazon* (New York: The John Day Co., 1952), p. 180.

In Japan the impact of the status oriented house can be followed clearly. The traditional house there varies little from subarctic Hokkaido in the north to subtropical Kyushu in the south, except for strength of frame, width of roof overhang, and, occasionally, the use of street arcades in the north. As the Japanese spread from south to north, they took with them the house identified with their culture; even the Ainu, the original inhabitants in the north, gave up their thick-walled dwellings for the fragile houses of their Japanese conquerors. I can affirm from personal experience how uncomfortable the Japanese house can be during the winter, even in relatively warm Honshu. This house, although comfortable during summer days, is closed up at night by shutters, making it very uncomfortable indeed. The shuttering is based on socio-cultural attitudes, notably a fear of "burglars" which is more superstitious than real.[9]

Europeans, and some natives, in North Africa insist on living in European style dwellings; the courtyard house would be much more comfortable, but there are questions of status and modernity involved. One reason why westerners have been unable to use such court dwellings is the scale and arrangement of spaces, which are *culturally* unsuitable.[10] Natives, on the other hand, have had to brick up openings in European houses, not only to avoid light and sun but also for privacy.[11]

Religious proscriptions sometimes create anticlimatic solutions, as is the case with the Chams, who regard shade cast by trees as unlucky, so that both houses and streets are exposed to the terrible sun and trees never planted. In Cambodia a similar lack of shade trees is brought about by the belief that it is unlucky for roots to find their way under the house.[12]

In Fiji, Malaya, and Japan, not only did Europeans often live in houses unsuited to the climate, but the relatively comfortable traditional houses are now being replaced with galvanized iron roofed (or, even worse, all metal) houses which are even less satisfactory. In the South Seas, European houses are a mark of power and good fortune, even though they are hotter and less well insulated than the traditional ones, and hence less comfortable.[13] In Japan thatch is being replaced by sheet metal, which is much less practical in both heat and cold, drips condensation, and rusts, yet is widely adopted because it is new.[14] In Peru,

---

[9] Bruno Taut, *Houses and People of Japan*, 2nd ed. (Tokyo: Sanseido, 1958), pp. 12, 70, 219-220. See also Pierre Deffontaines, *Géographie et Religions*, 9th ed. (Paris: Gaillimard, 1948), p. 28, where he contrasts the lack of heating in the Japanese house with the huge *Kang* (stove) in the Chinese house in areas of similar climate.

[10] See E. T. Hall, *The Hidden Dimension* (Garden City, N.Y.: Doubleday & Co., 1966), pp. 144, 151-152.

[11] Jean Gottmann, "Locale and Architecture," *Landscape*, VII, No. 1 (Autumn 1957), 20.

[12] Pierre Deffontaines, *Géographie et Religions*, p. 40.

[13] *Aspects de la Maison dans le Monde*, pp. 95, 97.

[14] Bruno Taut, *Houses and People of Japan*, pp. 70, 205. It is of interest to note that his remarks apply to as early as 1938. The process can still be observed today in Fiji, Malaya, South America, and elsewhere.

FIG. 2.1.   Typical open house in jungle near Iquitos, Peru.

FIG. 2.2.   House in Iquitos, Peru (native area of Belén). Note
use of solid walls for privacy, the major change from house in Fig. 2.1.

especially on the Altiplano, the status of galvanized iron is such that not only is it replacing both thatch and tile, to the detriment of comfort, appearance, and landscape, but the only way to get people to cooperate in a recent self-help school building project was to agree to the use of galvanized iron roofs—the status symbol. The visiting architects achieved comfort by concealing thatch in the ceilings.[15]

Despite these examples, it is a characteristic of primitive and vernacular buildings that they typically respond to climate very well. I am not trying to deny the importance of this variable, but merely to cast doubt on its determining role.

Materials, Construction, and Technology

"For thousands of years wood and stone have determined the character of buildings." [16] Present cultural attitudes make this statement a popular view, but its roots go far back in time. It has been widely used in architectural theory both in the past and today. The argument, put most simply, is that if it applies to high-style design, then these factors must become particularly strong in societies of limited technology and, hence, strong constraints.

In this view, forms develop as man learns to master more complex building techniques, and all forms are part of a progressive development in a series of almost inevitable steps. The cave—with no building—gives way to the windbreak, the circular hut, and finally the rectangular hut in its various forms which are, in turn, derived from the various materials and techniques available.

We have already seen that in Tierra del Fuego the windbreak is used for shelter, while more sophisticated forms are used for ceremonial buildings. The Southwest Pomo (Kashaya) Indians of California used the bark tepee, rather a primitive form, and the even more primitive temporary brush house, while their ceremonial buildings—sweathouses and elaborate roundhouses—have sophisticated roof structures. The roundhouse used to be semi-subterranean, possibly an archaic form comparable to the Kiva, but retains the same space organization, relationships, and basic form now that it is above ground and built of new materials; the central pole was actually moved from the old roundhouse to the new one.[17] This suggests that the form is at least partly independent of the materials and structural means employed, and that progress in the use of advanced techniques is not inevitable.

The determinist view neglects the *idea* of the house; just because man can do something does not mean that he will. For example, although the ancient Egyptians knew the vault they rarely used it, and then only

[15] Pat Crooke, "Communal Building and the Architect," *Architects' Yearbook 10* (London: Paul Elek, 1962), pp. 94-95.
[16] R. J. Abraham, *Elementare Architektur* (Salzburg: Residentz Verlag, n.d.), 3rd page of Introduction. My translation.
[17] Personal communication from a student at the University of California, Berkeley. Among the Paiute Indians we also find the whole range from open shelter and windbreaks to elaborate sweathouses.

where it could not be seen, since it was at odds with their image or idea of the building.[18] Primitive and vernacular building provides examples in which knowledge of technology does not mean that it will be used. In Haiti one can see very sophisticated woven planes, perfect for walls, leaning against some very crude houses, but used only for fishing traps, never for building.[19] The marriage *Scherm* of the Bushmen is more carefully built and larger than the regular house, although it is temporary; symbolism is apparently of more importance than utility.[20]

There are also situations where social values take precedence over technological advances. This is an interesting point, since we tend to equate technological advances with progress without thinking of the social consequences of adopting such advances. In North Africa the French piped water to a series of villages, which caused serious dissatisfaction. Investigation showed that in Moslem society women are shut in the house, and the village well provides their only chance to get outside, gossip, and see their limited world. As soon as the well was restored and the taps eliminated, the dissatisfaction ended. In some areas, after thatch has been replaced by more modern materials, it becomes fashionable as an antique with status value. As we have seen, galvanized iron can also become a symbol of success.

The fact that circular huts are easier to roof than rectangular ones need not be denied when we question the notion that change from one to the other responds to building skills only. The change of form may, in fact, be related to the symbolic nature of the two forms. Some peoples have both round and rectangular forms—as in the Nicobar islands—while others have never had round forms. For example, China, Egypt, and Mesopotamia have had rectangular houses all through recorded history, whether built of stone, mud, or other materials.[21]

Materials, construction, and technology are best treated as modifying factors, rather than form determinants, because they decide neither *what* is to be built nor its form—this is decided on other grounds. They make possible the enclosure of a space organization decided upon for other reasons, and possibly modify that organization. They facilitate and make possible or impossible certain decisions, but never decide or determine form. The Koelwai of Celebes have three different types of elevated dwellings of very different degrees of structural complexity.[22] The plans

---

18 Siegfried Giedion, *The Eternal Present,* Vol. 2, *The Beginnings of Architecture* (New York: Pantheon Books, 1964), pp. 514-515.
19 On a small island near the Ile à Vache off the south coast of Haiti near Les Cayes. I discovered this in some photographs taken by Mr. Alan Krathen, a student of mine.
20 See Raglan, *The Temple and the House,* p. 123. See also J. B. Jackson, "Pueblo Architecture and Our Own," *Landscape,* III, No. 2 (Winter 1953-54) 21 ff., where he points out (p. 21) that the Pueblo Indians could roof large Kivas but stuck to small rooms 7′ × 12′ × 20′. If they wanted more space, they used more than one room, so the pueblo became a multiplication of the basic unit. While the scarcity of timber undoubtedly played a role, it was not the determining factor, since piers could have been used if desired, as in Iran.
21 Deffontaines, *Géographie et Religions,* p. 17.
22 A. H. Brodrick, "Grass Roots," *Architectural Review,* CXV, No. 686 (February 1954), 110.

of the Eskimo igloo and tent are the same, although very different materials are used. Of course materials do make a difference, especially by making some procedures impossible. The Eskimo cannot very well build a snow igloo in the summer, when there is no snow. We should look for what a cultural or physical setting makes impossible, rather than for what it makes inevitable—a point of great importance in this book.

Materials in themselves do not seem to determine form. In Japan, thatch takes on many forms, sizes, and slopes.[23] The sizes of roof beams and roofs are related to their function as a status symbol, the wealth of the farmer, and the Japanese love of nature and hence of natural materials, sometimes at the expense of rational construction. In fact, the structure of the Japanese house has been said to be generally irrational.[24] All roofs in China are of tile, yet the forms within one village may differ greatly due to the influence of Feng Shuei (cosmic orientation—see Chapter 3). The pueblos are all built of the same materials and yet, considering only those enclosing plazas, we find very different forms—E shaped, oval, D shaped, round, rectangular, and so on.

All houses in the South Seas use the same basic technology—polished stone and shell adzes—and materials, yet their numerous forms differ greatly. While the tools used in Polynesia and Melanesia are the same, the houses are much grander in the former because of different social organization and prestige of ruling families. Similarly, in Papua-New Guinea the same materials and technology have produced very different forms.

Change of materials does not necessarily change the form of the house. On the Greek island of Santorini (Thera), a major innovation in materials has not affected form. Houses there were roofed with vaults built of stones laid radially, with mortar joints. In 1925 a master mason went to Athens, saw concrete, and on his return improvised a local lightweight concrete made of the volcanic soil of the island. Neither the form of the house nor that of the vault changed, however.[25] Similarly, it has recently been reported that the Mongol Yurt is now being built with plastic rather than the traditional felt covering, but that its form has remained unchanged in all respects. We have all seen, in our own culture, forms derived from one material executed in another; for example, wood churches imitating stone ones, and vice versa.

Frequently the same materials can result in very different forms, as shown by the examples in figures 2.3-2.6. There are also situations in which climatic needs have led to structurally nonoptimal forms, as in the Ashanti and Iranian huts (to be discussed later) with heavy walls

---

[23] Taut, *Houses and People of Japan*, pp. 110 ff. The slope varies from the flattest possible, 40° to 60°. See also Richard Weiss, *Die Häuser und Landschaften der Schweiz* (Erlenbach-Zurich: Eugen Rentsch Verlag, 1959), pp. 67, 68-69, where the slopes of roofs are the same for different materials and different for the one material—thatch. However, roof slope is an important and characteristic element and often used in classification.

[24] Taut, *Houses and People of Japan*, pp. 130-131, 217 ff.

[25] C. Papas, *L'Urbanisme et L'architecture populaire dans les Cyclades* (Paris: Dunod, 1957), pp. 143-144.

FIG. 2.3. *Dwellings made of one material (reeds). Left: Uru dwelling, Lake Titicaca, Peru. Right: Marsh Arab dwelling, Iraq-Iran border.*

FIG. 2.4. *Dwellings made of one material (mud). Left: Iran. Right: Pueblos, southwestern United States.*

FIG. 2.5. *Portable tents of sticks and felt. Left: Arab tent. Right: Mongol Yurt.*

FIG. 2.6. *Two examples from the great range of house forms using thatch and wood as materials. Left: Masai dwelling (Africa). Right: Yagua dwelling (Amazon). The houses in figures 2.3 through 2.6 are not drawn to the same scale, but their size is indicated by comparison with the human figure.*

and, especially, *roof* on a slender frame. In other cases the reasons for irrational structure may be religious or social. In any event, structural techniques and materials by themselves do not seem to fully explain the nature and diversity of the forms which we find.

Site

I am not certain that any consistent theory of site as a form determinant has ever been proposed. However, there have been attempts to explain the form of such *settlements* as Italian hill towns and towns and villages in the Greek islands—hence also house form—in terms of terrain, lack of land, and so on. There is the ecological determinism of Evans-Pritchard and others regarding the Nuer in the Sudan,[26] and the work of Brockmann in Switzerland attaching a great deal of importance to this aspect.

It would be wrong to minimize the importance of site for primitive and vernacular builders, but one can question the determining influence of the site on house form. The importance of site is shown by the almost mystical attachment of primitive, and even peasant, cultures to the land, testified to by the care with which land is treated and houses placed on it. This attachment can lead to persistence of sites because of their traditional nature. For example, the Southwest Pomo Indians of California have refused to leave a site which is unsatisfactory in terms of access to work and shopping because of its traditional nature;[27] in the past, when these same Indians moved from coastal locations in the summer to mountain ridges in the winter, their houses remained unchanged in spite of the very different sites.

In the southwestern United States, areas of similar site and climatic conditions have been the setting for both the highly individual Navajo house and the Pueblo cluster, which is basically a social unit the collective nature of which is essential. There are also profound differences between the landscape, settlement pattern, and house forms in Chihuahua (Mexico) and Texas, which are separated by the border, an imaginary line in physical terms, but very real in terms of attitudes to life, economics, nature, and the meaning attached to the house and the city.[28]

The *Hogaku* system of orientation in Japan determines the location of Japanese houses without regard to topography, while in India houses on steep hillsides are so strictly oriented to the East that the doors face

---

[26] See E. E. Evans-Pritchard, *The Nuer* (Oxford: Clarendon Press, 1960), pp. 57, 63-65; and Robert Redfield's criticism of this in *The Little Community* (Chicago: University of Chicago Press, 1958), pp. 30-31. See also Lucy Mair, *Primitive Government* (Harmondsworth, Middlesex: Penguin Books, 1962), pp. 22-25, where, in discussing the Nuer, Dinkah, Anuak, and Shilluk of East Africa, she attributes their settlement patterns almost exclusively to site, particularly to the need to avoid floods.

[27] There is also the example of the reconstruction of towns and villages on the same sites after wars, disasters, and so on, in spite of attempts to relocate them in more "reasonable" places.

[28] See J. B. Jackson, "Chihuahua—As We Might Have Been," *Landscape*, I, No. 1 (Spring 1951), 14-16.

up the slope.[29] In the Gilbert and Ellice islands houses are oriented to the forces of the Universe rather than to the topography,[30] as was also the case in China. Stones and hillocks have stronger earth powers than lowlands in Lithuania, so buildings are placed with consideration of this belief rather than in relation to topography in the physical sense. Non-use of land through the reservation of graves, groves of trees, historical sites, and sacred water sources is an important general aspect of the influence of site on house placement—but site in the spiritual, not the physical, sense.

The impact of site on crops is more critical than on house form, yet even crops in one particular area may change as they have done in Ceylon from spices to coffee, to tea, to rubber, and may change again. Of course, there are physical limits—one cannot grow pineapples in Greenland [31]—but there are many choices for any area. Similar site conditions can also result in very different house forms, and similar forms can be built on very different sites. Water, as a site, for example, can be handled by building over the water on pilotis, building on the shore, or using a floating house. Site makes some things *impossible*—one cannot have a floating house where there is no water—but all the forms have been used and all have variants.[32] At the same time, houses raised on pilotis have been used far from water, and in some cultures different groups of people on the same site use houses either on stilts or on the ground.[33]

Very similar sites often show very different forms; for example, on the coast one can aim for the view or turn away from it. Even sites as forceful as mountains, deserts, and jungles have produced great variations in house forms.[34]

As we have noted, site influences both the city and the house, but it does not determine form. We might say with Vidal de la Blache that "nature prepares the site and man organizes it to enable him to satisfy his desires and his needs." [35] In one sense, the effect of site is cultural

---

[29] David Sopher, "Landscape and Seasons—Man and Nature in India," *Landscape*, XIII, No. 3 (Spring 1964), 14-19.

[30] Peter Anderson, "Some Notes on the Indigenous Houses of the Pacific Islands," *Tropical Building Studies*, University of Melbourne (Australia), II, No. 1, 1963.

[31] L. Febvre, *La Terre et L'évolution Humaine* (Paris: La Renaissance du Livre, 1922), pp. 432-438.

[32] For example, see Rapoport, "Yagua, or the Amazon Dwelling," pp. 27-30, where houses in clearings in the jungle, on the shore, and floating are all described in the Iquitos area of Peru. See also G. Gasparini, *La Arquitectura Colonial en Venezuela* (Caracas: Ediciones Armitano, 1965), pp. 22-23, 33, 36, where we find that, on Lake Maracaibo and other lakes in the area, communal houses for 300 in clearings in the jungle, scattered dwellings in villages and hamlets on the shore, and lake dwellings on piles are all used.

[33] Deffontaines, *Géographie et Religions*, p. 23, referring to cultivators and craftsmen on the Admiralty Islands.

[34] Compare Max Sorre, *Fondements de la Géographie Humaine* (Paris: Armand Colin, 1952), pp. 202-206, with regard to site, altitude, and cities; and L. Febvre, *La Terre et L'évolution Humaine*, pp. 411 ff., where cities on similar sites (Zurich, Lucerne, Thonne, and Geneva; Venice, Amsterdam, Danzig) are shown to be very different.

[35] Cited in Febvre, *La Terre et L'évolution Humaine*, p. 414. My translation.

rather than physical, since the ideal site depends on the goals, ideals, and values of a people or period, and choice of the "good" site—whether lake, river, mountain, or coast—depends on this cultural definition. Use or nonuse of mountains may be due not to their difficulty as sites but to the attitude taken toward them.[36] Site selection may be due to supernatural aspects or may depend partly on the political and social viewpoint, as in Islam, where in some periods coastal sites were sought for cities, while in others inland locations were preferred.[37]

Within cities, preferred sites have varied in similar ways. Typical of Moslem cities is the location of "nobler" crafts immediately around the Mosque and "baser" ones further out, a pattern independent of the nature of the physical site. It was brought to Mexico by the Spaniards (who probably got it from the Arabs), and in the same area we find both Indian towns with a random distribution of trades and Spanish towns with the "Islamic" pattern of "noble" trades and rich houses clustered around the Plaza.[38] In one case position is significant and in the other it is not, a crucial element in the space organization of the house-settlement system (see Chapter 3), yet independent of site.

Settlement patterns themselves, which tend to great complexity, seem independent of site. The same areas may have isolated farms, hamlets, or villages, while even mountains, which are rigorous and forceful sites, exhibit a variety of habitats based on cultural grounds, as in dispersed Germanic areas and large villages in the Latin areas of the Alps.[39]

Mediterranean areas display a great concentration in villages, and a desire for concentrated living no matter what the site. An area like the Balkans shows historical, i.e., cultural, differences rather than those due to site or climate, and Greco-Roman, Turkish, Slavic, and other forms are often found in the same place. Sardinia has had very different village and house types at different times, as have parts of Africa.[40] In fact, almost universally, the same site through history will have had very different forms of dwellings, as is true of Latin America, where areas changed from Indian houses to courtyard houses with the coming of the Spaniards, and are now changing to the Anglo-American house-settlement pattern, as is also happening in the cities of Africa and Asia. The courtyard house itself was used on both flat and hilly sites, although some modifications did occur (Fig. 2.7).

[36] Deffontaines, *Géographie et Religions*, p. 101. For example, compare the Altiplano in Brazil and Peru, mountains in the Kabylie and Japan.

[37] Paper by Professor Charles Issawi, Columbia University, at the Conference on Middle East Urbanism, University of California, Berkeley, October 27-29, 1966. In relation to buildings see Vincent Scully, *The Earth, The Temple and The Gods* (New Haven: Yale University Press, 1962), pp. 22, 26, on how different sites were sought out in different periods.

[38] Dan Stanislawski, *The Anatomy of Eleven Towns in Michoacan*, The University of Texas Institute of Latin American Studies X (Austin: University of Texas Press, 1950), especially pp. 71-74.

[39] Sorre, *Fondements de la Géographie Humaine*, pp. 67 ff., 70. It should be stressed that both houses and settlements are *affected* by the physical site.

[40] *Ibid.*, pp. 73-76.

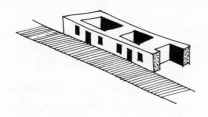 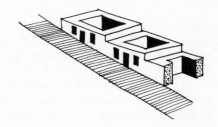

FIG. 2.7. Part of a row of courtyard houses (Latin America).
Left: Flat site. Right: Hilly site.

Defense

Typically, when social explanations of house form are proposed, defense and economics—the most *material* ones—are most commonly used. Defense has been cited more to account for tight urban patterns than to explain the form of dwellings, but even in this respect it does not provide a fully adequate explanation. Prehistoric Crete provides a good instance of an area where defense could not have been the reason for the tightly clustered settlements, which must be attributed to the gregarious instincts of the people. This gregariousness, which applies to the Mediterranean as a whole, still prevails today. There are few isolated farms in Crete, although there may be some isolated huts occupied during certain periods of the year. The Cretan's house is in the village, if possible.

The unsociable Englishman prefers to live near his work even if he has to walk miles to visit his neighbours, his pub or his chapel. The social Greek prefers to live in a crowded village among his friends and his cafe, even though he may have to walk miles to till his fields or trim his vines, and I think the prehistoric Cretan was like him.[41]

The compact towns in the Greek islands have been attributed to the needs of defense, lack of money (so that the houses themselves had to form the city wall), lack of arable land and the need to conserve it, and the need for shading for climatic reasons. Since all of these undoubtedly play a part, no single causation is possible; we need also to consider the element of choice, as exemplified by a love for crowding.

Defense certainly plays a role in deciding house form, and use of stockades, palisades, and fences has defensive implications as well as the religious ones discussed later. Defense, however, never fully accounts for form and may even be symbolic, as has been suggested for the Pueblos.[42] Even where defense is obviously of great importance, as among the Masai, the specific form of the dwelling is related to their

[41] R. W. Hutchinson, *Prehistoric Crete* (Harmondsworth, Middlesex: Penguin Books, 1962), pp. 161, 163.
[42] See J. B. Jackson, "Pueblo Architecture and Our Own," *Landscape*, III, No. 2 (Winter 1953-54), 23, where he suggests that it is not a fortress but exists to symbolically protect the sacred room.

attitude to cattle, which is a very different matter. The Masai warriors' kraal, which is also defensive, has a form very different from the "normal" kraal and no fence, while the Mousgoum farm in Tchad is also an enclosed circle for defense, a type of nomadic encampment in permanent form, but different from the Masai version.

In the Cameroons the need for defense is handled very differently because granaries rather than cattle are important, and there is a different value system. Within the same area of the Cameroons, where the danger of attack is relatively constant, the forms differ depending on whether the family is polygamous or monogamous. In each case there is concern with controlling access by use of a single entry, but the spatial arrangements vary depending on family and social organization. For example, in Douvangar Mofou and Foufou farms the entry is through the house of the head of the household, while on the Massa farm the chief is in the middle, surrounded by members of his family. The Natakan farm has defensive needs but its form is different because the family is monogamous; the woman has great authority and controls the main granaries. We therefore see marriage customs and other factors affecting the form of different dwellings, all of which have defense requirements.[43]

The communal dwelling has been linked by some to the need to form a survival unit.[44] Even if this explanation is accepted, we find that this form is not an inevitable result of the need for defense. The communal dwelling is a very different solution to the mountaintop village, or the village behind a palisade. Sparta and Athens found very different ways of handling the need for defense, as did Venice and the walled towns and even the latter can be very different in form—as are Carcassonne and Aigues Mortes. Communal dwellings themselves take on contrasting forms: the pueblo is very different from the Iroquois longhouse, which in turn differs from the Kwakiutl house. They vary in shape, size, and internal arrangement. For example, in Venezuela we can compare the round *churuata* of the Piaroa Indians in the Alto Orinoco with the rectangular collective house with curved apsidal ends of the Motilone Indians on the Venezuela-Colombia border; they also have different internal arrangements, the latter having three aisles. On the Brazilian border there is still another type in which, in addition to the three aisles, palm leaves divide the living areas.[45] We have already seen that both pile dwellings and other types coexist on Lake Maracaibo. The pile dwelling has an obvious defensive component against people, insects, animals, and snakes, yet other types seem able to solve the problem in

---

[43] See Beguin, Kalt et al., L'habitat au Cameroun (Paris: Publication de l'office de la recherche scientifique outre mer, and Editions de l'Union Française, 1952) for many examples of the variations in the houses of the Cameroons.

[44] Deffontaines, Géographie et Religions, p. 114, relates it rather to totemic clan structure, while Lewis H. Morgan gives it a very different attribution, and comments on the great number of forms the communal dwelling in North America takes in his Houses and House Life of the American Aborigines (originally published 1881; republished Chicago: University of Chicago Press, Phoenix paperback, 1965). The communal dwellings of New Guinea and Oceania generally are, as we have seen, religiously motivated.

[45] Gasparini, La Arquitectura Colonial en Venezuela, pp. 20-21, 22, 23, 35, 36.

the same area. Access to pile dwellings varies greatly—boats or bridges are used when the houses are over water, while those on land employ ladders which can be withdrawn, or types of access ladders which animals cannot negotiate, such as notched tree trunks or the pole steps of the Congo.[46]

Some villages in Slovakia have a "defense" form while others do not.[47] Survival of an archaic form in some areas and its disappearance in others which are adjacent show the complexity of the forces operating. The inception of the fortified house, found from the Atlas Mountains to Scotland, is often not for defense in the direct sense, and the forms taken are very different. We need only compare the houses of the Atlas with those of Scotland, or the towers of San Giminiano or Bologna with the Palazzi of Florence. The towers of Bologna and San Giminiano themselves are not just a defensive form—matters of prestige are involved, and other towns in the area did not develop that form.

In summary, many factors are neglected by accepting defense as the only determinant of form. Additionally, the element of *choice* of which method of defense is to be used is of great importance.

Economics

Economics has been widely used to explain settlement and building form, and its importance is indeed great. However, it is possible to question its determining role through an argument analogous to one already used. In an economy of scarcity the need to survive and to use resources maximally is so great that these forces may be expected to wield tremendous power. If, even under those conditions, economic forces are not dominant, then the argument for economics as generally determining form becomes rather suspect.

Even in economies of scarcity there are many examples of herders living among agricultural people and not only failing to accept the economy available, but despising it and the people who practice it. The Babenga and the Pygmies exchange agricultural products and game without giving up their way of life.[48] The Masai, Bakitara, and Banyankoli in East Africa avoid the economic possibilities of the examples around them, and use their cattle unwisely in economic terms because of the

---

46 Pile dwellings have been explained in terms of climate—they aid ventilation—and site—they help avoid flooding; they also help fishing, water supply, and waste disposal, and have even been given a religious explanation, once again demonstrating the complexity of the form determinants. Tree dwellings, which are used in a number of countries, such as Melanesia and Central India, seem to be primarily for defense purposes, but there may also be religious and mystical components involved.

47 I. Puskar and I. Thurzo, "Peasant Architecture of Slovakia," *Architectural Review* (February 1967), 151-153.

48 Febvre, *La Terre et L'évolution Humaine*, p. 302. An analogous situation with regard to housing is the action of the Anglo-Saxons, who did not live in the luxurious empty Roman villas which they found; they destroyed them and built their rather primitive wooden huts close by. See Steen Eiler Rasmussen, *London: The Unique City*, 3rd ed. (Harmondsworth, Middlesex: Penguin Books, 1960), p. 22.

social and religious importance of cattle.[49] Since the Masai also have a horror of permanent dwellings, schools had to be installed in the open air and missionaries encountered a good deal of trouble in getting the idea of a permanent church accepted.[50]

Such people hardly ever consider giving up their way of life. When it *is* given up it may be exchanged for a "lower" economic level, as when the Cheyenne, with the introduction of the horse, gave up their permanent villages of semisubterranean houses and became nomads living in tepees; they gave up agriculture for the hunt. This is a reversal of the almost biological evolution from the tent to the hut and then the house, and also a reversal in economic terms according to early evolutionist views. From this point of view the Hidatsa, mentioned earlier, are of interest because their two ways of life, one of which had at one time been regarded as more advanced than the other, coexist, as do the corresponding house forms. In fact, archaic survivals are as common in economic life as they are in house forms.

Since houses are less critical for survival than food, we would expect them to be even less affected by sheer economic necessity. In Annam, as soon as a peasant has money he builds a house, beautiful but not comfortable, and *beyond his means;* there are more rich houses there than rich families.[51] Generally, since people with similar economies may have different moral systems and world views, and since the house is an expression of the world view, economic life has no determining effect on house form. Even lack of labor specialization, so typical of primitive, and to a lesser extent vernacular, builders, may be socially and culturally rather than economically motivated, and specialized labor may be despised. Even collaborative building may be due not to economic needs or complexity of task, but be socially motivated. An example is the Cebuan dwelling in the Philippines, which would be more economical if built differently, but social cooperation, good will, and community are the dominant factors.[52]

As we have already come to expect, the same forms of economy (in agriculture, for example) may lead to widely differing forms of rural settlement, houses, and their spatial arrangement. Wine growing areas

[49] See H. Epstein, who points out many instances of noneconomic values being dominant in the domestication of animals in his "Domestication Features in Animals as a Function of Human Society," in *Readings in Cultural Geography,* eds. Philip L. Wagner and M. W. Mikesell (Chicago: University of Chicago Press, 1962), pp. 290-301. Such values are held by many other people; for example, the Toda of South India. See also Deffontaines, *Géographie et Religions,* pp. 197-198, 229 ff., and Redfield, *The Little Community,* p. 25.

[50] Deffontaines, *Géographie et Religions,* p. 77, fn. 4. The Bedouin despise city dwellers and have a "mystical hatred of the roof, a religious revulsion to the house." See also Jer. 35: 5-10, on the Rechabites who must not build houses and always live in tents.

[51] Deffontaines, *Géographie et Religions,* p. 16.

[52] D. V. Hart, *The Cebuan Filipino Dwelling in Caticuyan* (New Haven: Yale University Southeast Asian Studies, 1959), p. 24. See also Robert Redfield, *The Primitive World and Its Transformations* (Ithaca, N.Y.: Cornell University Press, 1953), p. 11, where he disagrees with V. Gordon Childe about cooperation being economic in nature and quotes Polanyi on "economy submerged in social relations" and, in fact, says that in primitive and precivilized societies economy is chiefly noneconomic.

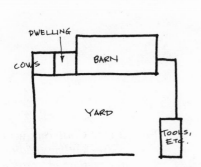

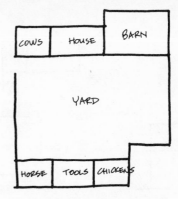

FIG. 2.8. *Diagrammatic plan of a typical French farm with yard.*

FIG. 2.9. *Diagrammatic plan of a typical Italian farm with yard.*

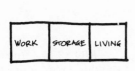

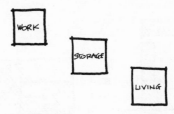

WORK, STORAGE & LIVING UNDER ONE ROOF

SEPARATION OF WORK, STORAGE & LIVING

FIG. 2.10. *Two basic patterns of the division of elements in farm dwellings. (Adapted from Weiss,* Häuser und Landschaften der Schweiz.*)*

in France show both concentrated and dispersed settlement patterns, while the cave houses of the Loire Valley growers are very different from the houses of Provence.

Demangeon, who regards the French farmhouse as an economic tool and attributes its form to the need for man, his goods, and animals to be close together,[53] fails to account for the great variety of ways in which this goal is met. It is of interest to examine some farmhouses comprised of the same elements, and to see how differently they handle the requirements.

In the North of Italy, almost the same elements produce a plan very different from the French farmhouse (figs. 2.8, 2.9), while Swiss farmhouses show many arrangements of the economically required elements—house, stable, and threshing floor (Fig. 2.10) falling into two basic patterns, within which are innumerable variants. They differ from Demangeon's examples, although the elements remain the same.[54]

[53] A. Demangeon, "La maison rurale en France—essai de classification," *Annales de Géographie* (September 1920), pp. 352-375.
[54] Richard Weiss, *Die Häuser und Landschaften der Schweiz,* pp. 176-177, 179, 184-186, 189, 198, 236, 243 ff. See also Sorre, *Fondements de la Géographie Humaine,* pp. 135, 139.

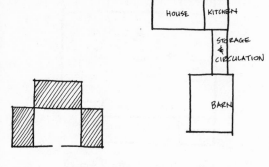

INCA MARCA

NEW ENGLAND FARM

FIG. 2.11. *Clustering within free outline (additive) as a method of providing space differentiation in dwellings and farms.*

ANCIENT GREECE

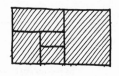

AUSTRIAN FARM (TYROL)

FIG. 2.12. *Internal division within fixed outline (subtractive) as a method of providing space differentiation in dwellings and farms.*

All of these house complexes demonstrate a general aspect of the economic need to *store,* especially in the rural house. This need affects the Inca house and the Pueblo as much as the French farmhouse, as shown by their clustering, but the *form* of that clustering differs and indicates the importance of considering the specifics of the problem rather than only its general features. If it is accepted that vernacular building is additive and adapts to changes more readily than the closed forms of high-style design, all these variations then fall into one of two ways in which additions can be made. One is by clustering, as in the pueblo, Inca *marca,* Italian and French farmhouses, and the New England farmhouse (Fig. 2.11). The other method is through inside subdivision, as in the Ancient Greek house or certain Swiss farms where growth was by subdivision within the wall rather than by addition (Fig. 2.12).

One factor which might be involved in all these variations is some aspect of social organization which differs among societies with otherwise similar economic bases. Once again, however, this does not fully account for the differences. For example, the extended family may account for the occurrence of grouping, but not for the form that it takes. The collective group of the Slavic countries, the *Zadruga,* is very different from the Kabylie collectivity and the Arab form generally; the Southwest Pomo Indian groupings of California are very different from those of the Pueblos, and both of these are very different from the Iroquois of the longhouse.

36

Even nomads, for whom the economic base affects house form by imposing the need for *mobility*, use widely varying forms. The Yurt of the Mongols, the hexagonal tent of the Tibetans, the numerous forms of the Arab tent, and the tepee and substantial, yet mobile, wooden houses of the Indians of the Pacific Northwest are all very different. Apparently even so critical an aspect of economic life as mobility does not suffice to account for house *form*, although it exerts great constraints.

The houses of the seminomadic slash and burn (swidden type) agriculturalists of the tropical forests, who have to move periodically because of rapid soil exhaustion, vary from very large communal houses of various kinds to small individual houses. Since these are all people of similar economic activity, their differing house forms reflect the different ways in which they visualize the setting for life. Figures 2.13-2.20 compare seminomadic dwellings and settlements. The settlement patterns are not drawn to scale, and they are based mostly on verbal descriptions. The houses are drawn to a common scale, and they, too, are based mostly on verbal descriptions.

Even in the case of modern American buildings, where the economic aspects would seem to be dominant, it has been pointed out that the

SETTLEMENT PATTERNS   HOUSES

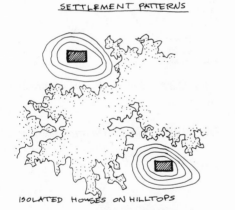

ISOLATED HOUSES ON HILLTOPS

FIG. 2.13. Meo (Southeast Asia).

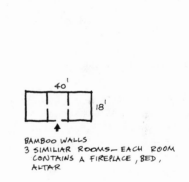

BAMBOO WALLS
3 SIMILAR ROOMS— EACH ROOM
CONTAINS A FIREPLACE, BED,
ALTAR

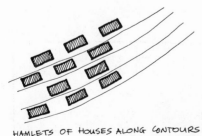

HAMLETS OF HOUSES ALONG CONTOURS

FIG. 2.14. Man (Southeast Asia).

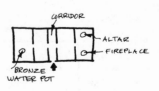

VILLAGES MAY MERGE - IF THEY
DO, THEN THE BORDER IS AT A
"PALAUER" HOUSE WHICH EACH
VILLAGE POSSESSES

FIG. 2.15. Fang (Africa).

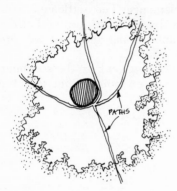

IN CLEARING IN JUNGLE

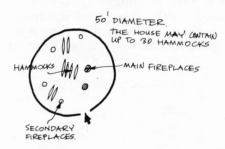

FIG. 2.16. Piaroa (South America).

FIG. 2.17. Jamadi (South America).

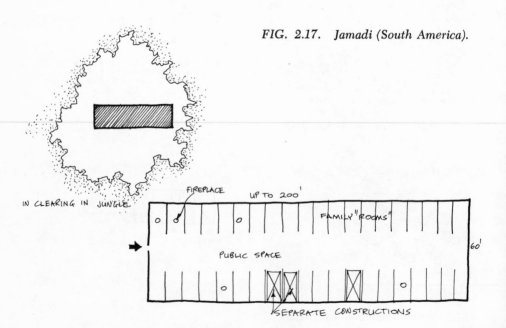

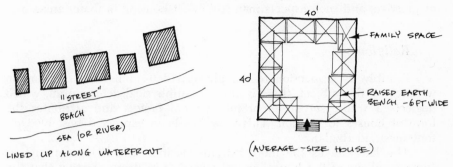

FIG. 2.18.   *Kwakiutl (northwest North America).*

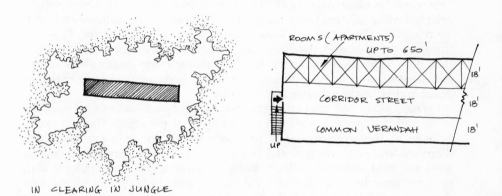

FIG. 2.19.   *Dyaks (Borneo).*

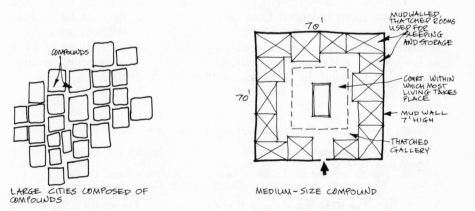

FIG. 2.20.   *Yoruba (Africa).*

rise of the skyscraper in nineteenth century Chicago had no economic justification at the time, because of foundation problems and other factors.[55] The fact that every town wants a tall building is also a matter of prestige, and such aspects may still affect housing in many areas.

Religion

Possibly as a reaction to the physical determinism so common in writings on the subject, there is also an antiphysical determinism, which neglects a whole set of important material factors and attributes the form of houses to religion. This view has been expressed best by Deffontaines and Raglan.[56]

The latter takes the more extreme position which he sums up as "the sacredness of the house"[57] and succeeds in demonstrating that the house is much more than shelter. It becomes clear that this alternate view explains many aspects of the house at least as well as the physically oriented view of the house as shelter. However, the religious view is oversimple in trying to attribute everything to a single cause. It is one thing to say that the dwelling has symbolic and cosmological aspects, that it is more than a device for "maintaining the equilibrium of the metabolism," and another to say that it has been erected for ritual purposes and is neither shelter nor dwelling but a temple.

Once again the general point, even if accepted, fails to account for form, and the specifics need to be considered. If we accept that the house belongs to the woman and is primarily related to her, and that man therefore visits the woman and her bed,[58] the actual forms and devices used are very different indeed. Religion alone cannot account for this, so there must be other forces involved—a view strengthened by the fact that even today there are differences in the men's and women's domains in the American and English house.[59] Similarly, the sacredness of the threshold and portal, and hence the separation of the sacred and profane realms, can be achieved through the use of numerous and varied forms.

Deffontaines does refer briefly to the action of material forces, and is therefore more balanced than Raglan. However, because he concentrates on the religious aspect alone, and brings an overwhelming amount of material to support his view that religion is the determinant of form in landscapes, settlement patterns, cities, houses, demography, cultivation, and circulation, he presents a rather distorted view.

---

[55] Martin Meyerson, "National Character and Urban Form," *Public Policy* (Harvard) XII, 1963.

[56] Deffontaines, *Géographie et Religions*, who also deals with the impact of religion on all aspects of geography; Raglan, *The Temple and the House*. See also Mircea Eliade, *The Sacred and the Profane* (New York: Harper & Row, 1961).

[57] Raglan, *The Temple and the House*, Chap. 1 and p. 86.

[58] *Ibid.*, p. 35 ff.

[59] E. T. Hall, *The Hidden Dimension* (Garden City, N.Y.: Doubleday & Co., 1966), p. 133.

His view that while both man and animals seek shelter, a place to
store things, and a micro-climate, only man has a spiritual aspect which
is uniquely human and which distinguishes his constructions from nests,
beehives, and beaver dams, is very convincing.[60] Many examples can
be found of this sacred function of the house. In some cultures a man
exiled from his house was separated from his religion, and for many
peoples—in ancient Rome, New Caledonia, Cambodia, Annam, and
China—the house was the only temple. Not only was the house the sole
temple for daily (as opposed to official) religion for the ancient Chinese,
but everything about it was sacred—roof, walls, door, fire, and well.
There are areas such as Cambodia where allowing strangers into the
house would be sacrilege; in Africa the house is primarily spiritual, a
link among man, his ancestors, and the earth, and the principal inhabitants of many houses are the invisible, extranatural and supernatural
beings. For nomads the tent is the dwelling of the divinity (which may
explain the horror of houses noted before), and it is usually surrounded
by a fence which delimits semisacred ground (such as the *Zeriba* of the
Berbers); the fence may be as much for the separation of sacred and
profane as for defense.[61]

Religion affects the form, plan, spatial arrangements, and orientation of the house, and may be the influence which leads to the existence
of round and rectangular houses. The reason for a culture never having
had round houses may well be due to the needs of cosmic orientation—
a round house cannot easily be oriented. In Africa the distribution of
round and rectangular houses is related to the distribution of religion,
and many examples can be found, like the Zulu, where orientation is
unimportant, round houses are used, and there may not be any straight
lines. An extreme contrast is the *Trano* of Madagascar, which is oriented
through strict axes and astronomical rules.

Many other aspects of the house—whether it is on stilts or underground, whether it needs special provision for keeping out or controlling
evil spirits—can be attributed to religion. Similarly, the impact can be
shown of religious considerations on settlement patterns and their changes
in a given area. The Chinese village, the existence of ritual villages—as
in the New Hebrides or the Sunday villages of Brazil and Guatemala—
can be much better understood if the religious factor is considered. It is
the only factor which would explain the special underground houses for
menstruating women, as, for example, among the Nez Perce Indians.

It would be wrong, however, to say that all these aspects of dwellings
have been determined by this single variable. This oversimple, almost
determinist, approach is the greatest weakness of a view which provides
insights which seem more significant than those of physical determinism.
We begin to see that everything, including the house, can assume sym-

[60] *Ibid.*, pp. 12, 15-16.
[61] Deffontaines, *Géographie et Religions*, pp. 16-17. See also *Aspects de la Maison
dans le Monde*, p. 14; the common practice of excluding menstruating women from
the house also suggests its sacred nature.

bolic significance—that the whole Cosmos is a potential symbol.[62] Since there is a choice of symbols, religion as an explanation of house form is more possibilist, and less determinist, than the physical explanations of form.

General Criticism of the Physical Determinist View

The preceding section suggests that, before proposing an alternative way of looking at house form, a discussion of the determinist position in general, and the physical determinist view in particular, may be in order. This discussion seems called for in view of the great variety of consequences that can result from seemingly similar causes, and the similar results that seem to flow from totally different causes.

Cultural geography in general has seen a movement away from physical determinism. Deffontaines's book as a whole can be taken as questioning the determinist position, in that he points out that most primitive and even preindustrial peoples stress religion, in the broadest sense, more than they do material considerations or even comfort. This is a useful reaction against a view which says that "primitive architecture can be explained wholly in these material factors," being strictly utilitarian.[63]

Sorre points out that a meaningful civilization arose on the Northwest Coast of North America, but not in Tasmania or on the west coast of South America, which provided the same physical milieu.[64] The possibilities were the same, but since possibilities have to be used *there can be no physical determinism*. In fact, the school of geography represented by de la Blache, Febvre, Sorre, and Brunhes has been called "possibilist" because of its stress on the fact that the physical setting only provides possibilities, not imperatives, and it is man—not site or climate—that decides. This applies to many aspects of cultural geography and economic life, as well as to the dwelling and settlement. The great variety of forms strongly suggests that it is not site, climate, or materials that determine either the way of life or the habitat. Many examples from almost all areas of the world could be adduced to show that dwellings and settlements are not the result of physical forces, particularly since the form often changes in areas where physical aspects have not changed.

A good starting point in any general questioning of the physical determinist view is Mumford's argument that man was a symbol-making animal before he was a tool-making animal, that he reached specialization in myth, religion, and ritual before he did in material aspects of culture, and that ritual exactitude came before exactitude in work; man put his energy into symbolic rather than utilitarian forms even when he was barely starting. Possibly a nonphysical position needs to be taken

---

[62] Carl Jung, *Man and His Symbols* (Garden City, N.Y.: Doubleday & Co., 1964), p. 232.
[63] Sir Herbert Read, *The Origins of Form in Art* (New York: Horizon Press, 1965), p. 99.
[64] Sorre, *Fondements de la Géographie Humaine*, Vol. 3, p. 11.

regarding primitive house forms, since song, dance, and ritual were more advanced than tools.[65]

From this point of view, man's achievements have been due more to the need to utilize his internal resources than to his needs for control of the physical environment or more food. Mumford posits the primacy of the symbol—the primacy of the poetic and mythic function of symbols rather than their rational or practical use. This may explain the great variety of languages in such primitive areas as Aboriginal Australia or New Guinea. The primacy of this mythic function becomes clear from a comparison of the art of Lascaux and Altamira with the technology of the time—something which must have struck every visitor to these places.[66]

A similar contrast of approaches occurs if we compare Redfield's view of prehistory with Gordon Childe's. Redfield stresses the primacy of what he calls the moral order over the technical order in primitive societies, and questions Childe's rather materialistic approach, which stresses technique. Early societies, Redfield points out, are largely ethical, and their moral order is stronger than their technical one.[67]

I have already commented on the highly developed ceremonial life among people with poor material cultures. It might be interesting to determine how much time primitive people actually spend on ceremonial activities and ritual.[68] Of course, primitive and peasant people regard *most* activities as ceremonial in nature. In many cases, what distinguishes these people from each other is not their material life—which tends to vary little—but their ceremonial, and this is inevitably reflected in their buildings, as I will try to show in Chapter 3. For example, in New Guinea the *Kona* tribe, stone age and very primitive, has such a complex religious and ritual life that special villages needed for the ritual dances are built according to a specific plan (Fig. 2.21).[69]

The South Seas, the poverty of which has often been stressed, displays great stress on ceremonial avenues in the villages, and the vast men's houses with their dance grounds. These houses built for major rituals are very large and elaborate, often more than 300 feet long, with

[65] Lewis Mumford, *Art and Technics* (New York: Columbia University Press, 1952), and "Technics and the Nature of Man," in *Knowledge Among Men*, ed. S. Dillon Ripley (New York: Simon and Schuster, 1966). E. R. Service, *The Hunters* (Englewood Cliffs, N.J.: Prentice-Hall, Inc., 1966), p. 2, contrasts the simplicity of hunting cultures with respect to technology with their complexity with respect to etiquette, religion, art, family, friendship, and kinship rules, which may be more complex than the corresponding institutions in our culture.

[66] As far back as excavations go, evidence of religious activity is found, and houses and tents show evidence of foundation sacrifices and other rituals. Many peoples will not enter a house or tent until it has been consecrated. See, for example, *Archeologia* (Paris), No. 4 (May-June 1965), pp. 18 ff., describing a dwelling at the cave of Salpêtrière, 20,000 years old, where ceremonies took place both at the erection and taking down of the tent. The excavators speak rather touchingly of the people staying out longer in the blinding storm while the consecration went on.

[67] See Redfield, *The Primitive World and Its Transformations*, and V. Gordon Childe, *What Happened in History* (Harmondsworth, Middlesex: Penguin Books, 1961).

[68] In fact E. R. Service, *The Hunters*, p. 13, remarks on how little time primitive people spend on food-gathering and related activities, and also on their complex and ritual food-sharing system.

[69] *Aspects de la Maison dans le Monde*, pp. 58-59, 65-66.

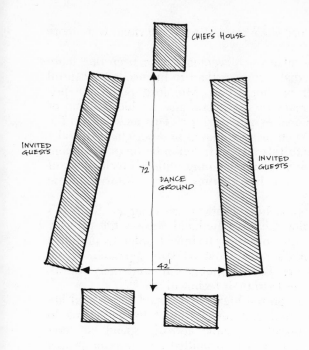

FIG. 2.21. *Diagrammatic plan of special village for dance rituals, Ronpila, New Guinea. (Adapted from* Aspects de la Maison dans le Monde, *p. 66.)*

FIG. 2.22. *Men's ceremonial greathouse and woman's dwelling, Kalaba tribe, New Guinea. Each area has a different type of greathouse— all are different but equally grand.*
(Adapted from photograph in Guiart, Arts of the South Pacific, *p. 42.)*

44

different roof forms and details and elaborate entry porches (Fig. 2.22). Inside there may be two sides accommodating two intermarrying groups, each side having its own hearth and as many compartments as there are patrilineal groups in the community, and different grades of members may also have different compartments.[70] Each compartment stores the cult objects of the group, and at the far end is a walled-off area in which particularly sacred objects are stored, and is accessible only to the leading men of the village.

The fact of more stress on the symbolic than the utilitarian in these areas of low, almost subsistence, economy suggests that when there is an economy of abundance and surplus this emphasis becomes even more possible—but there is no inevitability, merely possibility. The exclusive, or inevitable, action of cultural factors is equally as untenable as any other single determinant and we need to recognize a valid middle ground. The need to consider many factors is, in the final analysis, the main argument against any determinist view. Societies of wealth may be able to devote their surplus to symbolic objectives, but may not wish to, as their value scales change and symbolic values become less important than they were in poorer societies. In the latter, however, striking instances of the value attached to symbols may be found, as in the case of the Eskimo woman who, in 1772, was trying to survive as a castaway all by herself. When found, she had produced art objects, decorated her clothing, and so on; while the Eskimo has had to reduce life to the barest essentials, art and poetry are an essential part of that life.[71]

[70] Guiart, *Arts of the South Pacific*, pp. 35-36, 38, 132.
[71] See E. Carpenter in G. Kepes, ed., *Sign, Image, Symbol*, p. 206.

CHAPTER 3 *socio-cultural factors and house form*

The Basic Hypothesis

The different forms taken by dwellings are a complex phenomenon for which no single explanation will suffice. All possible explanations, however, are variations on a single theme: people with very different attitudes and ideals respond to varied physical environments. These responses vary from place to place because of changes and differences in the interplay of social, cultural, ritual, economic, and physical factors. These factors and responses may also change gradually in the same place with the passage of time; however, lack of rapid change and persistence of form are characteristic of primitive and vernacular dwellings.

The house is an institution, not just a structure, created for a complex set of purposes. Because building a house is a cultural phenomenon, its form and organization are greatly influenced by the cultural milieu to which it belongs. Very early in recorded time the house became more than shelter for primitive man, and almost from the beginning "function" was much more than a physical or utilitarian concept. Religious ceremonial has almost always preceded and accompanied its foundation, erection, and occupation. If provision of shelter is the passive function of the house, then its positive purpose is the creation of an environment best suited to the way of life of a people—in other words, a social unit of space.

The limited value of the classification of forms, or even the analysis of economy, site, climate, materials, and technology has already been discussed. Both physical and socio-cultural aspects need to be considered, but the latter need primary stress. Once the identity and character of a culture has been grasped, and some insight gained into its values, its choices among possible dwelling responses to both physical and cultural variables become much clearer. The specific characteristics of a culture—the accepted way of doing things, the socially unacceptable ways and the implicit ideals—need to be considered since they affect housing and settlement form; this includes the subtleties as well as the more obvious or utilitarian features. It is often what a culture makes *impossible* by prohibiting it either explicitly or implicitly, rather than what it makes inevitable, which is significant.

Given solutions or adaptations do not always occur simply because they are possible. The physical setting provides the possibilities among which choices are made through the taboos, customs, and traditional ways of the culture. Even when the physical possibilities are numerous, the actual choices may be severely limited by the cultural matrix; this limitation may be the most typical aspect of the dwellings and settlements of a culture.

My basic hypothesis, then, is that house form is not simply the result of physical forces or any single causal factor, but is the consequence of a whole range of socio-cultural factors seen in their broadest terms. Form is in turn modified by climatic conditions (the physical environment which makes some things impossible and encourages others) and by methods of construction, materials available, and the technology (the tools for achieving the desired environment). I will call the socio-cultural forces primary, and the others secondary or modifying.

Given a certain climate, the availability of certain materials, and the constraints and capabilities of a given level of technology, what finally decides the form of a dwelling, and moulds the spaces and their relationships, is the vision that people have of the ideal life. The environment sought reflects many socio-cultural forces, including religious beliefs, family and clan structure, social organization, way of gaining a livelihood, and social relations between individuals. This is why solutions are much more varied than biological needs, technical devices, and climatic conditions, and also why one aspect may be more dominant in one culture than it is in others. Buildings and settlements are the visible expression of the relative importance attached to different aspects of life and the varying ways of perceiving reality. The house, the village, and the town express the fact that societies share certain generally accepted goals and life values. The forms of primitive and vernacular buildings are less the result of individual desires than of the aims and desires of the unified group for an ideal environment. They therefore have symbolic values, since symbols serve a culture by making concrete its ideas and feelings. At the same time, house forms, more than other artifacts, are influenced and modified by climatic forces, choice of site, and availability and choice of materials and construction techniques.

In this context, socio-cultural forces can be seen in many different ways. The term *genre de vie* used by Max Sorre includes all the cultural, spiritual, material, and social aspects which affect form. We can say that houses and settlements are the physical expression of the *genre de vie*, and this constitutes their symbolic nature.

I would further suggest that the socio-cultural component of the *genre de vie* is the sum of the concepts of *culture, Ethos, world view,* and *national character* used by Redfield, which he defines as follows:

Culture—the total equipment of ideas and institutions and conventionalized activities of a people.
Ethos—the organized conception of the Ought.
World View—the way people characteristically look out upon the world.
National Character—the personality type of a people, the kind of human being which, generally, occurs in this society.[1]

It is the sharing of a world view and other image and value systems which makes possible the process of vernacular building described in Chapter 1, as well as the successful relationships between buildings which are the topic of urban design.

Various attempts to explain forms and relations through physical and technological needs and constraints lose sight of the fact that even these forces, constraints, and capabilities are themselves the result of the cultural climate which preceded the material or visible change. A house is a *human* fact, and even with the most severe physical constraints and limited technology man has built in ways so diverse that they can be attributed only to *choice,* which involves cultural values. Within the various economic and geographical constraints, the biological, physical, and psychological makeup of man, and the laws of physics and structural knowledge, there are always numerous choices available, particularly since man has a great "propensity to symbolize everything that happens to him and then react to the symbols as if they were the actual environmental stimuli." [2] Socio-cultural forces, therefore, become of prime importance in relating man's way of life to the environment.

In discussing the reasons for the forms of houses and settlements, it may be useful to think of them as a physical embodiment of an ideal environment. This is suggested both by the long history of the ideal city and by the fact that the Iroquois, for example, used their longhouse as a symbol, calling themselves the people of the longhouse.[3] The house may also be considered as a physical mechanism which reflects and helps create the world view, ethos, and so on, of a people, comparable to the various social institutions (or mechanisms) which do the same. For example, education can be regarded as reflecting cultural attitudes and helping to mould the ideal man,[4] the family as a device to transmit and guard the ethos and form national character through the ideal man, and religion as defining the ethos. In the same way, the house and the settle-

---

[1] Robert Redfield, *The Primitive World and Its Transformations* (Ithaca, N.Y.: Cornell University Press, 1953), p. 85. Copyright 1953 by Cornell University. Used by permission of Cornell University Press.
[2] René Dubos, *Man Adapting* (New Haven: Yale University Press, 1965), p. 7.
[3] L. H. Morgan, *Houses and House Life of the American Aborigines* (originally published 1881; republished Chicago: University of Chicago Press, 1965), p. 34.
[4] Its ideal may be either to preserve the traditional ethos or to encourage change. See Margaret Mead, "Our Educational Goals in Primitive Perspective," *American Journal of Sociology,* XLVIII (May 1943), 9.

ment may serve as physical devices to perpetuate and facilitate the *genre de vie*.[5] In this interpretation the house is not purely a physical thing.

The idea of the house as a social control mechanism, so strong in traditional cultures at least, may no longer apply with as much force in a society with the formalized and institutionalized control systems of today. Under such conditions the link between culture and form is weakened, and it may no longer be possible to destroy a culture by destroying its physical setting.[6] This link never fully disappears, however, and the house and its use still tells the young much about life and the attitudes expected of them, such as formality, informality, and neatness; the "silent language" still speaks.[7]

Creation of the ideal environment is expressed through the specific organization of space, which is more fundamental than the architectural form and is closely related to the concept of the *Ethnic Domain*.[8] This can be defined as the ideal environment made visible; it is basically nonphysical in inception and is given manifest form through buildings. An example is the way the pueblo is built to protect the sacred room in the center, reflecting the way corn is planted.[9] Reasons for the great number of house types not easily understood in the context of relatively few climatic types, limited number of materials, or other physical factors, become much clearer if viewed as expressions of ideal environments reflecting different world views and ways of life.

It is the sometimes subtle influence of these forces which affects the way we behave and how we *wish* to behave, the clothes we wear, the books we read, the furniture we use and *how we use it*, the food we eat and *how* we prepare and eat it, and consequently the houses and settlements in which we live and how we use them. It is these influences that make it easy to identify a house or city as belonging to a given culture or subculture.

Socio-cultural Forces and Form

In denying the determining nature of religion, I wanted to make clear that it is not a universal or inevitable characteristic, merely one of the cultural choices possible. Since religion forms an essential part of

---

[5] An example is the array of devices developed in Japan to relieve the tensions generated by crowding and by the hierarchical structure of Japanese society, with its web of obligations, elaborate ritual of etiquette, and suppression of emotions. These devices are both social—demonstrations, acceptance of drunkenness (a drunk is by convention invisible to public and police)—and physical—the geisha house and, above all, the *Inn* which can best be understood in these terms. See John Fischer in *Harper's* (July 1966), 18.

[6] See the case of the Bororo village described by Claude Lévi-Strauss, *Tristes Tropiques* (Paris: Librairie Plon, 1955), pp. 228-229.

[7] The term is E. T. Hall's.

[8] Susanne Langer, *Feeling and Form* (New York: Charles Scribner's Sons, 1953), pp. 92 ff., esp. p. 95.

[9] J. B. Jackson, "Pueblo Architecture and Our Own," *Landscape*, III, No. 2 (Winter 1953-54), 23.

most primitive and preindustrial cultures, it forms a suitable starting point of this discussion of the forces leading to the symbolic nature of buildings. This discussion can best begin by our considering the impact of the cosmic image on form in general.

The Cosmos may be reflected in a microcosm at a whole range of scales, from an entire land through a city, a village, a house as a whole, the space within a house, and the furniture in it. Each, or all, may reflect the shape in which the world is visualized.[10]

At the largest scale the all-pervasive influence of the Cosmic Image can be seen in Africa, where in general the sacred is very important, traditional values are not questioned, the symbolic load of artifacts, buildings, and indeed the whole land is very great, and the order of society, the order of thought, and the order of the Universe are in close correlation.[11] Among the Dogon and Bambara of Mali every object and social event has a symbolic as well as a utilitarian function. Houses, household objects, and chairs all have this symbolic quality, and the Dogon civilization, otherwise relatively poor, has several thousand symbolic elements. The farm plots and whole landscape of the Dogon reflect this cosmic order. Their villages are built in pairs to represent heaven and earth, and fields are cleared in spirals because the world has been created spirally. The villages are laid out in the way parts of the body lie with respect to each other, while the house of the Dogon, or paramount chief, is a model of the universe at a smaller scale. Multistoried houses are the prerogative of the highest religious and political leaders and are symbols of power, representations of them being used for many purposes; for example, as masks to frighten away the souls of the dead.[12]

At the scale of the city, the layout of the Indian town, according to the Manasara Silpa Sastras, is based on the "cosmic cross," the cardinal points of which are the corners of the universe; the whole town and its temple are symbolic of the celestial city. The symbolic view affects not only the form of cities but their founding, and applies, for example, to China, Inca Peru, Africa (e.g., Ghana and Egypt).[13]

[10] See Robert Redfield, *The Little Community* (Chicago: University of Chicago Press, 1958), p. 87, on the four-cornered universe of the Maya, which can be compared with the circular universe of the Sioux.

[11] Georges Balandier, *Afrique Ambiguë* (Paris: Librairie Plon, 1957), pp. 2-3, points out that traditional African thought is symbolic rather than discursive, and that Negro civilizations are often richer in symbolic than in material productions. Through the ritual and symbols one can tell much about a society.

[12] Exhibition at the Kroeber museum, University of California, Berkeley, March, 1967. After death an altar is built on the roof of the house, and the souls of the dead stay close to the relatives, showing the sanctity of even ordinary houses. The souls are then persuaded to leave by the use of the masks.

[13] See Mircea Eliade, *Cosmos and History: The Myth of the Eternal Return* (New York: Harper & Row, 1959), pp. 4, 90; also *The Sacred and the Profane* (New York: Harper & Row, 1961), pp. 20-67. Eliade points out that for primitive man the only "real" events are mythological ones. These become the models and, by a "paradigmatic gesture," make the nonsacred real (pp. 31, 45, 65). See also Paul Wheatley, "What the Greatness of a City Is Said To Be," *Pacific Viewpoint*, IV, No. 2 (September 1963), pp. 163-188, regarding the city as *imago mundi* with the cosmogony as the paradigmatic model and the importance of these aspects in the layout of cities; A. F. Wright, "Symbolism and Function," *Journal of Asian Studies*, XIV, No. 4 (August 1965), pp. 667 ff., who points out that the city is a model of the Cosmos.

We find very much the same attitude reflected in the village. The placement of Pawnee villages in relation to each other was always a replica of the stars in the sky, while for the Hottentots the circle is the perfect form which brings down heaven's blessings. The huts are round and arranged in a circle around the circular cattle ground. The chief's house is always so precisely in the spot of the rising sun that one can tell from its location at what time of year the camp was set up. The other houses are arranged in a hierarchic order in the direction of the sun's movement.[14]

A similar form is found in European peasant cultures: the *Solskifts*, or solar villages of the Baltic countries, also reproduce the daily path of the sun. The main street is oriented North-South, with houses on both sides arranged in order starting on the west side. The numbers go from south to north on the west side and from north to south on the east side, like the movement of the sun. The best spot is Number One, which is for the most honorable house. The façades of the houses always face the street and always get either the east or west sun. A similar system applied to the fields, and while it broke down because of excessive rigidity it is still found in Sweden, Finland, Denmark, and Yorkshire (brought by the Danish invasions).[15]

It is clear that the form of houses in a village like this would be greatly affected, if only through orientation. Ritual orientation of the house, which is found in many cultures, is a function of cultural and religious attitudes rather than material factors. Even when the two coincide, as with the Feng Shuei system of China, which is sometimes related to comfort, comfort will have to give way if it is at odds with the religious aspects. This system is closely related to the whole culture and, through the rules of geomancy, governs the direction of roads, and watercourses, the heights, forms, and placement of houses, and the placing of villages and graves in the mystical environment among the fortunate forms of trees and hills. The central values of the people relate to these cosmological beliefs.

Success, which is important for Cantonese peasants, is believed to relate to supernatural forces, and the orientation of settlements and houses to aspects of the environment is essential, since these lucky supernatural forces need to be tapped for good fortune. The whole complex theory can be summarized for our purposes by saying that these forces flow like water from the hills, and the power of the clan is increased if one can tune in to them. Groves of trees act like filters and are planted first; building may wait until the trees are tall enough. The forces are made to flow into the ancestral hall, and the whole process is the responsibility of experts. The roof forms in various parts of the village depend on the relation of the building to the forces. The layout of rooms inside the house and even the placement of furniture inside a room are also affected. The relation of the movement of evil spirits to straight lines

---

[14] Pierre Deffontaines, *Géographie et Religions* (Paris: Gallimard, 1948), p. 118.
[15] *Ibid.*, pp. 118-119. See also Plate 10 (Munster, North Bavaria) for an example of such a village.

leads to roads, bridges, and entries to houses which are not straight, and entrances never face in unlucky directions.[16]

A similar system, introduced from China, was used in Japan. Because of it, superb views might be ignored and faced by a toilet, because an entrance, kitchen, or toilet must *never* be placed on a north-east or south-west axis. As late as the 1930's houses planned by diviners used these rules, codified in special diagrams with 24 cardinal points which give good and bad directions separated by as little as 7 or 8 degrees.[17]

The house itself was a microcosm in primitive and preindustrial cultures, as the city was an *imago mundi*. The Pawnee earth lodge, for example, is regarded as typical of man's abode on earth, where the floor is the plain, the wall the distant horizon, the dome the arching sky, and the central opening the zenith, the dwelling of the invisible power.[18]

An indication of the symbolic nature of the house is the fact that so many immigrants bring their architecture with them, and persist in its use even though it is often unsuitable for the new area in which they live. The symbolic character is important to them, however; it is a piece of *home,* and hence familiar in symbolic terms.[19]

In the Marquesas, as in most of Oceania, the climate is mild, and simple shelter often all that is needed. The traditional practice, however, was for five or six families to have three buildings on a five-foot-high stone platform which took more time to build than the houses. However, it was essential to be above the ground. The rear house was a dormitory for all the people, while the others were a house for meals (taboo to women) and a kitchen (Fig. 3.1). In this case taboo determined the need for the differentiation of space.

The Samoan house exhibits the minimum need for shelter which the climate suggests, and the religious influence is less dominant. The house is round, possibly for symbolic reasons, and consists of a circle of columns and a conical roof. The floor is distinguished from the outside realm by being covered with a different material—crushed coral wetted with water. Insect protection is given by mosquito nets hung from strings which traverse the house (Fig. 3.2). Several families live in such a house, which is merely a differentiation of space from the outside

---

[16] Dr. J. M. Potter, Dept. of Anthropology, University of California, Berkeley. This system is still in use in Hong Kong today, where I have seen it applied to a new office building in 1965.

[17] Bruno Taut, *Houses and People of Japan* (Tokyo: Sanseido Co., 1958), p. 29, diagram, p. 30, p. 31.

[18] Lord Raglan, *The Temple and the House* (New York: Norton, 1964), p. 138. On pp. 135-152 and elsewhere Raglan gives many examples. Of interest is the use of the analogy of the creation of the world in terms of building a house both in the Rigveda (p. 139) and in Ancient Greece.

[19] See N. R. Stewart, "The Mark of the Pioneer," *Landscape,* XV, No. 1 (Autumn 1965), 26 ff.; *Architecture in Australia,* LV, No. 6 (November 1966); letter from R. N. Ward in *Architectural Review,* CXLI, No. 839 (January 1967), 6, where he discusses the mineral discoveries in South Australia in the 1840's and the arrival of the Cornish miners to work them. "Their cottages were very strictly on Cornish patterns—and quite unsuitable that was for the Australian climate." See also Charles Cockburn, "Fra-Fra Houses," *Architectural Design,* XXXI, No. 6 (June, 1962), pp. 229 ff.

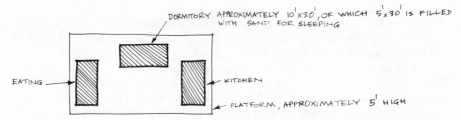

FIG. 3.1.   *Diagrammatic plan of Marquesas dwelling.*

FIG. 3.2.   *Samoa dwelling, diagrammatic plan and perspective.*

realm,[20] a place to store things, and a shade for siesta. The Marquesas (and Borneo) climatically demand a house of this type, yet structures there are much more elaborate and complex, a difference due to religious and other cultural factors.

In Polynesia the effect of religion, through the concepts of *mana* and taboo, is very strong. Food is often eaten outside or on special porches in order not to contaminate the house with *mana,* and for the same reason may be cooked in special ovens for chiefs and other special people. The chiefs are generally of great religious significance and their houses are very large and fine, as much as 150 to 300 feet long and 75 to 150 feet wide, built on raised stone platforms. The majority of people live in small rectangular huts. I have already mentioned that chiefs' houses are built by specialists, whereas the others are built by their inhabitants.

Even at the more advanced level of peasant societies, ceremonial is still of prime importance, and all social relations are more than utilitarian and always surrounded by symbolism. The omnipresent ceremonial must be paid for in labor, goods, or money, and the "ceremonial fund" in a peasant village may be very large compared to other aspects of the economy. The emphasis on ceremonial varies in different cultures. Its importance is related to its function in underlining and exemplifying the solidarity of the community; it also presents an ideal model of the

20 Related to the general importance of the threshold, which divides two sorts of space—the sacred and the profane—with the house as the center of the world (see Raglan, *The Temple and the House,* p. 142, citing Eliade, and pp. 144-145).

social mechanism. This is reflected in the attitude taken toward possessions which are never seen in their economic context alone. For example, a piece of land and a house are loaded with symbolic value, and are not merely factors of production.[21]

Inside the dwelling, symbolic attitudes account for the prevalence of symbolic space distribution in the house, courtyard, or tent—there seems to be no physical basis. A few examples, all of which are the result of hierarchies in the use and allocation of space, may clarify this point.

With regard to dining, the medieval pattern, involving hierarchic position along the table, is preserved in the Oxford and Cambridge colleges in England and is still found in peasant houses in Switzerland (Fig. 3.3) and elsewhere. This system involves a very strict seating order.[22]

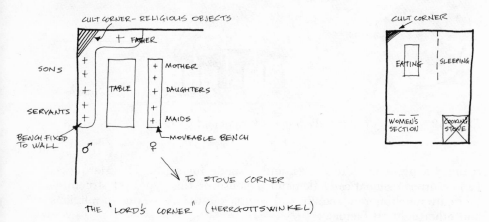

FIG. 3.3.   *This arrangement is almost unvarying throughout eastern and central Europe. The cult corner is the most important part of the house, which may explain the seating. (Adapted from Weiss,* Häuser und Landschaften der Schweiz, *pp. 151-152.)*

The prevalence of sacred or privileged corners or sides is almost universal. In Fiji the east wall is for the chiefs.[23] In China, although the whole house is sacred, the northwest corner is the most sacred.[24] The Mongol Yurt is divided into four parts: to the right of the door the husband and wife, facing them the guest of honor, and to the left the other guests in descending order of importance. The altar is always on the left of the bed as one enters.[25] In the Arab tent there is also a ritual

21 See Eric Wolf, *Peasants* (Englewood Cliffs, N.J.: Prentice-Hall, Inc., 1966), pp. 7-8, fn. 7, pp. 15-16. He points out that when this ceremonial aspect is given up, that is an indication of the breakdown of the society.
22 See Richard Weiss, *Häuser und Landschaften der Schweiz* (Erlenbach: Eugen Rentsch Verlag, 1959), pp. 151-152. The Sherpas of Nepal also have this, and there is a constant reseating going on, as people enter and leave, to maintain this hierarchy. See Von Fürer-Heimendorf, *The Sherpas of Nepal* (Berkeley and Los Angeles: University of California Press, 1966), p. 286.
23 Raglan, *The Temple and the House,* p. 108.
24 *Ibid.,* p. 128.
25 See G. Montell, *Journal of the Royal Anthropological Institute,* 1940, p. 82, cited in Raglan, *The Temple and the House,* p. 9.

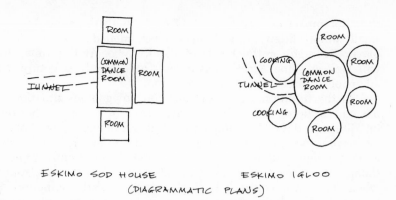

FIG. 3.4.   ESKIMO SOD HOUSE   ESKIMO IGLOO
            (DIAGRAMMATIC PLANS)

space distribution which differs among tribes; as one example, the entry in the Touareg tent is always on the south, with the men on the east side and women on the west.[26] This ritual space distribution is found in houses in India, in Lapland, and among the Northwest Indians. The most complex is the Madagascar house already mentioned.

The internal division in this house is according to the stars, with 12 divisions corresponding to the 12 lunar months. Each division has a different use, such as rice or water jar storage, according to religious prescriptions which also affect the furniture arrangement; the bed, for example, is always in the east, with its head to the north. The main façade with the door and windows faces west, since west is the principal direction, the people call themselves "those who face the West," and the house is closely related to the religious plan of the universe.[27] The north is the entry for notable visitors, the northeast corner is the most sacred, and the north wall is the place for the ancestor cult. If someone is to be honored he is invited to take the north place.

The radial plan of the Eskimo, which is the most characteristic feature of their dwelling, is closely related to the ceremonial and hierarchic aspects of the dance. The private rooms open off a dance room, and the plan is found in the sod house as well as the Igloo (Fig. 3.4).

At the scale of furniture, one can show that various pieces of furniture have religious and cosmological significance in different societies.[28]

I will now examine the influence on house form of other specific socio-cultural forces, primarily family structure, kinship, and caste.

Many examples in relation to family structure could be used to

---

[26] Kaj Birket-Smith, *Primitive Man and His Ways* (New York: Mentor Books, 1962), p. 142.
[27] Deffontaines, *Géographie et Religions*, pp. 18-19, 27, 29. Note that there is some relation to climatic comfort in some of these arrangements, but this is not the principal rationale. On pp. 21 and 23 he gives examples of more advanced cultures—Latvia, Holland, France—where the plans of houses reflect religious beliefs, which in many cases are now unknown but whose influence is retained.
[28] See Raglan, *The Temple and the House*, pp. 126 ff., esp. pp. 128, 132, on the *bed* as a microcosm of the cosmos; also p. 108, on the *table*. See also C. P. Fitzgerald, *Barbarian Beds* (London: Cresset Press, 1965), on similar aspects of the *chair* in China.

show its impact on house form: Oceania, with the men's houses and the small, simply fitted women's huts where men do not feel at home, the Slavic *Zadruga*, or the house of the Kabylie. At this time, however, I will look at some African examples where family structure, as well as other social forces, clearly affects form.

In the traditional African house, in polygamous situations, the man has no real house and visits his wives, each of whom has her own house, on different days. The impact of this arrangement on house form is clear when we compare two houses in the same area, one belonging to a polygamous and the other to a monogamous family (Fig. 3.5). Although the same features are found—separation of man from the wife whom he visits, controlled, single entry, walled compound, and protection accorded the granaries—the spatial arrangements are very different. In some areas, such as Ghana, the changes in the houses of one tribe can be traced as some of its members adopt Christianity, and with it monogamy.

In order not to oversimplify, it should be pointed out that other forces act at the same time, leading to different house forms among polygamous peoples. For example, in the case of the Foulbé, in the Cameroons, the man's position is expressed by his place being in the center of the compound, surrounded by his wives (Fig. 3.6). Here the

FIG. 3.5. *Comparison of Cameroon houses, both drawn to the same scale. (Adapted from Beguin, Kalt et al., L'habitat au Cameroun, pp. 19, 52.)*

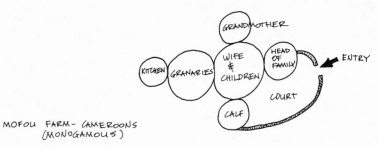

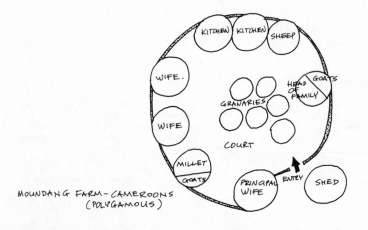

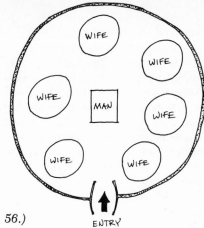

FIG. 3.6.   Foulbé farm—Cameroons.
(Adapted from L'habitat au Cameroun, p. 56.)

ENTRY

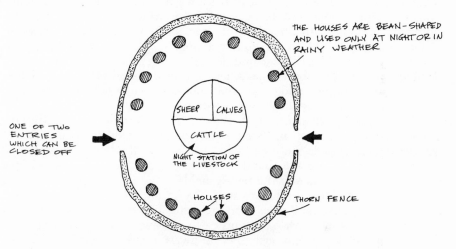

THE HOUSES ARE BEAN-SHAPED
AND USED ONLY AT NIGHT OR IN
RAINY WEATHER

ONE OF TWO
ENTRIES
WHICH CAN BE
CLOSED OFF

SHEEP   CALVES
CATTLE
NIGHT STATION OF
THE LIVESTOCK

HOUSES

THORN FENCE

FIG. 3.7.   Masai compound (diameter approximately 130 ft).

situation may become rather complex, with various subareas having separate controlled entrances, differing degrees of privacy, areas for guests, and so on, which can produce a rather labyrinthine quality.[29]

Finally, one can compare the Moundang, already discussed, with the Masai. The Moundang value granaries highly, and these are placed in the center of the compound. To the Masai, cattle are not only wealth but have mystical, religious, and ceremonial importance transcending their economic value and forming the basis of Masai culture. The compound is centered on them, with consequences of a very different scale and other changes in spatial organization (Fig. 3.7). The settlement pat-

[29] See Beguin, Kalt et al., L'habitat au Cameroun (Paris: Publication de l'office de la recherche scientifique outre mer and Editions de l'Union Française, 1952), for many examples. See also the chiefs' compounds among the Yoruba, the Fon, and elsewhere.

tern reflects this concern with cattle and the need to keep and guard them, and there are probably symbolic features in the circularity, the centrality, and the fence itself. The kraal is composed of an elderly father, wives, and married sons, and migrates as a unit; even the nomadic pattern itself is modified by the family organization and social goals. As is common, each wife builds her own hut, and the man sleeps in the hut of the wife whom he is visiting. At one time there were also warrior kraals composed of young men. Their social organization was very interesting, but significant for our purpose is that these kraals had no thorn hedges, and other variations in their physical form reflected specific social differences.

The influence of kinship and caste as the prime social influences can be seen in Cochin, South India, and as a result the village here has little social unity. Caste distinction results in a low community spirit in these villages. The arrangement also shows the importance of religious sanctions and a contempt for manual work which could not exist in primitive cultures, with their lack of specialization, and which are rare in peasant cultures. Only the gods and rich landholders have substantial houses. Lesser householders and tenant farmers live in simpler houses of mud brick, while laborers, artisans, and most of the population, who have no group property and no internal cohesion, live in one- or two-room huts of mud, bamboo, palm leaves, or straw.

In a typical settlement, the houses of the well-to-do Brahmans and Nayars stand apart, each in its own compound, loosely grouped around temples and ceremonial bathing tanks. The huts of the low caste artisans form one or more separate hamlets, while those of the agricultural laborers are scattered among the paddy fields.

The houses of the Brahmans and Nayars are laid out according to the religiously sanctioned rules for that caste. The compound is divided into four sections by north-south and east-west lines. The house occupies the northeast, or less propitiously the southwest, quadrant, burial grounds and cowsheds are in the southeast quadrant, and the bathing tank and sheds in the northwest. The house itself is of four blocks around an open rectangular court, with a verandah on all sides. Here also strict rules prevail—the west block is for sleeping quarters and stores, and the north for kitchens and dining. The east and south blocks open to the court, and only there are visitors and guests received.

Criticality and Choice

The suggestion that social and cultural factors, rather than physical forces, are most influential in the creation of house form is an important reason for turning to primitive and vernacular building for a first look at house form.

The more forceful the physical constraints, and the more limited the technology and command of means, the less are nonmaterial aspects able to act. However, they never cease to operate. This relationship suggests a set of scales along which buildings may be examined. We may posit a climatic scale ranging from very severe to very benign; an economic scale from bare subsistence to affluence; a technological scale from the barest skills and capabilities to their maximum; and a scale of materials ranging from the presence of a single local material to the existence of virtually unlimited choice. If it can be demonstrated that even where the most severe constraints of climate, economics, materials, and technology operate we still find great variations, choice, lack of determinism, and clear operation of cultural factors, we could conclude that the latter, in fact, would be the prime ones where a greater degree of freedom was present. We may say that *house form is the result of choice among existing possibilities—the greater the number of possibilities, the greater the choice—but there is never any inevitability, because man can live in many kinds of structures.*

It could be argued that whereas constraints in the past were climate, limited technology and materials, the forces of tradition, and lack of economic surplus, today's constraints are different but no less severe. Current constraints are those imposed by density and population numbers, and the institutionalization of controls through codes, regulations, zoning, requirements of banks and other mortgage authorities, insurance companies, and planning bodies; even today the freedom of the designer as form-giver is rather limited. Nevertheless, the *degree* of choice open to a builder in the United States today is very different from that available to an Eskimo or Peruvian peasant. The fact is that a degree of freedom and choice exists even under the most severe conditions, as we have seen repeatedly.

The possibility of this degree of choice and freedom with regard to the house, even under the maximum degree of constraint, is most usefully understood through the concept of *criticality*. The forms of houses are not determined by physical forces and hence can show great variety because of the relatively low criticality of buildings. This is the crucial argument: because physical criticality is low, socio-cultural factors can operate; because they can operate, purely physical forces cannot determine form.[30]

The concept of criticality can best be illustrated with some comparative examples. In problems of flight, a rocket has higher criticality than an airplane, because it is more severely constrained by technical requirements;[31] slow speed airplanes have more degrees of freedom, i.e., lower criticality, than rapid ones (compare the variety of forms in the 1920's with the relatively few forms of present day jets). A pedestrian path has much more design freedom than a freeway, which is constrained by passing distance, sight distance, radii, curves, size in relation to location, and many other technical considerations. However, even in this case there is a degree of choice depending on the value system, most funda-

---

30 We have also seen that even more critical aspects of life—economy, food, domestication of animals—have degrees of freedom of choice and "irrational," culturally based decisions.

31 However, a space capsule considering re-entry problems still has nine possible solutions, i.e., there is *choice*. See Peter Cowan, "Studies in the Growth, Change and Aging of Buildings," *Transactions of the Bartlett Society* (London: Bartlett School of Architecture, 1962-1963), p. 81.

mentally in the initial decision as to whether it should be built. In this sense the physical criticality of buildings is low, and one could argue that this low level of physical criticality gives more importance to cultural, social, and psychological factors.

In denying physical or economic determinism, I do not wish to substitute a form of cultural determinism.[32] I am arguing for the primacy, not the exclusive action, of socio-cultural forces. As the criticality increases along the different scales—climatic, economic, technological, or material—the degree of freedom, although decreased, persists, and is expressed under any conditions to the maximum extent possible. There are always many forces operating in combination. Man may build to control his environment, but it is *as much* the inner, social, and religious environment as the physical one that he is controlling—the ideal environment in cultural terms. He does what he wants as much as the climate will allow; he uses the tools, technology, and materials to come as close as possible to his ideal model. The relative dominance of various modifying factors is as much a function of the people's attitudes to nature as of the forcefulness of the factors; the degree of use of resources and technology is affected as much by goals and values as by their availability.

These choices, and the criticality, will result in varying dominance of one or another of these variables. It is for this reason that one must find the "flavor" of a culture's true meaning and beliefs before one can understand its houses.

Basic Needs [33]

The over-all concept of *genre de vie*, while useful in general terms, does not help us to determine how it affects the forms of dwellings and settlements. For that purpose it is necessary to break it down into terms even more specific and concrete than the concepts of world view, ethos, national character, and culture, because the lack of criticality in house form means that the same objectives can be met in many different ways, and that *how* a thing is done may be more important than *what* is done. This is logical if we accept the symbolic nature of man's environment, as well as evidence on the importance of symbolic values in many aspects of man's life and activity. The concept of basic needs is then brought into question, since all, or most, of them involve value judgments and therefore choice, even in the definition of utility. The very decision on the building and location of a freeway involves value judgments on the relative importance of speed and the beauty of a location, and is hence cultural, as is the decision to build a supersonic jet. A culture can stress utility, however defined, as the principal component of its world view, the way other cultures stress religion, and similar distinctions can be made concerning the value of comfort and other "needs."

---

[32] One could not if one wanted to; we have seen the very different forms that, say, communal living can take.
[33] I have used this concept, which I had arrived at independently, for a number of years, but have since discovered a similar position in L. Febvre, *La Terre et L'évolution Humaine* (Paris: La Renaissance du Livre, 1922), pp. 287 ff.

If we accept shelter as a basic need (and even this can be questioned), and also accept that the *idea* of the house, as opposed to shelter, comes very early, as recent discoveries show, then the form the house takes depends on how "shelter," "dwelling," and "need" are defined by the group. This definition will be reflected in the different interpretations given to such concepts as "home," privacy, and territoriality. In the same way, if we accept protection from weather and human and animal enemies as basic needs, the way in which this protection is achieved is open to wide choice, although always involving physical, psychological, and cultural limits. What is characteristic and significant about a culture is this choice, the *specific* solution to certain needs which, while they depend on interpretation, tend to be fairly widespread: the expression of one's faith and philosophy of life, communication with one's fellows, and protection from climate and enemies.

If the physical criticality of dwellings is low and fits to physical requirements not very critical—as shown by the way people can use old buildings and towns with very minor changes—then the concept of basic needs may be questioned. One could speak of them in terms of the need to breathe, eat, drink, sleep, sit, and love, but this tells us very little; what is important with regard to built form is the culturally defined way in which these needs are handled. It is not whether there will be a window or door, but their form, placement, and orientation which are important; it is not whether one cooks or eats, but where and how.

The following are some of the more important aspects of the *genre de vie* which affect built form:

1. Some basic needs.
2. Family.
3. Position of women.
4. Privacy.
5. Social intercourse.

Since each of these provides many choices of definition, relative importance, and forms used to provide for them, which depend on the goals and values of the culture or subculture, they need to be made very specific.

1. SOME BASIC NEEDS. While looking at basic needs in general terms tells us very little, it may be of interest to view them in specific terms. If we consider something as basic as breathing in specific terms, we become aware of its complex effect on built form. For example, in regard to fresh air or smells, the Eskimo accepts very high smell concentrations inside the Igloo, and the smell of the toilet is accepted in the traditional Japanese house.[34] There are also cultures where smoke is

---

[34] Taut, *Houses and People of Japan*, p. 38, expresses surprise at how people with such high aesthetic standards can accept this. In the United States the bathroom and toilet are very important. See Alexander Kira, *The Bathroom* (Ithaca N.Y.: Cornell University Center for Housing and Environmental Studies, Research Report No. 7, 1966), p. 7, for the lengths to which Americans will go to avoid odors.

sacred and is encouraged in the house.[35] There is a difference between attitudes to open windows in England and the United States and the fear of "night air" in some cultures, all of which affect the form of the house. Similar differences apply to the dark, with some cultures, like the Bamileke, wanting the house dark for cult purposes.[36] Desired light levels vary greatly from culture to culture, even between England and the United States, although one would think that visual tasks would result in constant light levels. Similar differences between these two cultures occur in the comfort level of heating, and we have already seen the difference in attitude to heating between China and Japan, and the effect on the house.

This last point suggests that even a concept such as *comfort*, which we take for granted, is less obvious than one would think, not only in what is regarded as comfortable, but even in the expressed need for comfort. For example, the Incas admired toughness and were scornful of comfort, which they equated with effeteness, while the Pueblos had a very different attitude.[37]

We have already seen how religious sanctions can affect eating and cooking habits, and there are many other examples of specific eating requirements greatly affecting house form. In the Aztec house the kitchen was a separate building, the Incas cooked out in the open court, and the Touareg had a fire in the tent for warmth, but cooked outside.[38] The rules of caste in India influence eating habits and architectural requirements, while in other cultures the dominant factor may be other food taboos [39] and purity and cleanliness requirements, such as provision for ritual washing of hands before a meal; among the American Indians it was the rules of hospitality, the habit of having one meal a day only, and the custom of men eating first, and women and children later.[40] The Chinese practice of the family eating together, and the Japanese one of men eating first and women and children later, also affected the form of their houses. We thus see that the basic need of eating does not say much about form—we need to know the specific manner of how and where eating and cooking are done.

The specific manner of gaining a livelihood is an important aspect of dwelling form, and even the concept of poverty varies among different

[35] Deffontaines, *Géographie et Religions*, pp. 29-30.
[36] *Ibid.*, p. 32.
[37] Consider also the difference between Sparta and other Greek cities. For an interesting discussion on the different types of comfort see William H. Jordy, "Humanism in Contemporary Architecture: Tough and Tender Minded," *Journal of Architectural Education*, XV, No. 2 (Summer 1960), 3-10.
[38] Raglan, *The Temple and the House*, p. 47.
[39] See Deffontaines, *Géographie et Religions*, pp. 20-21. The different food taboos among totemic people may require separate utensils, kitchens, and even granaries for man and wife, as among the Dobu of the Entrecasteaux archipelago.
[40] L. H. Morgan, *Houses and House Life of the American Aborigines*, pp. 44-45. These are three out of five aspects that he considers as social factors influencing house form. See also Deffontaines, *Géographie et Religions*, p. 20. Among the Ulufs of Senegal the man has his own house where he eats alone and in secret because he is afraid of being given the evil eye.

cultures. I have already referred to the lateness of economics, and it has been pointed out that "poverty" has a different meaning in traditional Japan than it has for us. The Japanese have no word for it in the sense of pity.[41] It is interesting to speculate as to what extent this is related to the simplicity, almost poverty, of Japanese aesthetics, hence the "empty" house, lack of possessions, and different space use of the Japanese house. If we compare a traditional Japanese room with a Victorian room or a contemporary American one, can we really conclude that basic needs have changed that much?

Sitting is a basic need, yet some cultures rest by squatting, as is common in Asia, others stand on one foot, as do Australian aborigines and some Africans, and it could be shown that the manner of sitting can affect house form and change living habits. Consider, for example, the impact of the introduction of the chair, which would revolutionize living habits and have major social consequences: the need to take off shoes, imposed by the use of mats, would disappear, hence also the special covered space—porch or verandah—where they are taken off and left; the need for shoes which are easily taken off would be eliminated, and also the need for special floors. Different postures would affect stance, carriage, costumes, the character and shape of all other furniture, and the use of cupboards, wardrobes, mirrors, lamps, and pictures.[42] The chair would also affect the sitting height, hence changing the placement and type of windows and the type of garden. Similarly, with regard to sleeping, it is not the fact of sleeping which is significant, but the furniture, arrangements, and spaces used which affect the house.

2. FAMILY. Although the family is basic, there are great differences in family structure [43] which are significant in relation to house forms which differ equally as much. Even when we have described the basic type of family structure, there may still be various forms that result, as, for example, the extended family group which can lead to the courtyard cluster of the Kabylie, the longhouse of the Iroquois, and the grouping of the Southwest Pomo of California, whose arrangement is not clear from the plan, and can only be seen once the names of the families are known (Fig. 3.8).

In the Kabylie each house shelters a conjugal family; the group of houses around its common court shelters the extended family and is the unit of the village. This may have been affected by the Islamic model where the town is broken up into a series of separate quarters along ethnic lines, within which are the separate clan groupings each with its own territory.[44]

---

[41] Taut, *Houses and People of Japan*, pp. 53, 64.
[42] C. P. Fitzgerald, *Barbarian Beds*, pp. 1-3.
[43] See A. M. Arensberg and S. T. Kimball, *Culture and Community* (New York: Harcourt, Brace and World, Inc., 1965), for a good summary of different types of family structure.
[44] See R. Maunier, *La construction de la maison collective en Kabylie* (Paris: Institut d'ethnologie, 1926), pp. 14 ff., 23. G. E. von Gruenebaum, "The Muslim Town," *Landscape*, I, No. 3 (Spring 1958), 1-4.

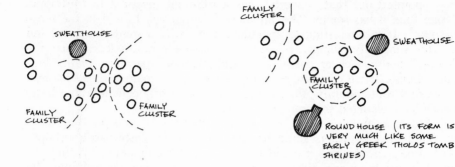

FIG. 3.8. *Grouping of Southwest Pomo Indians, California.*

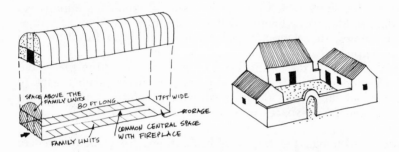

FIG. 3.9. *Left: Onondaga–Iroquois longhouse. (Adapted from*
Morgan, Houses and House Life of the American Aborigines, *p. 129.)*
Right: Inca marca *(for diagrammatic plan see Fig. 2.11). There are still*
great numbers of this type in the altiplanos of Peru and Bolivia.

The Iroquois longhouse is just one of many forms of the communal
house. Its specific form can be compared with that of the pueblo or the
Inca *marca* (Fig. 3.9).

We have already seen how house form differs between areas with
polygamy and monogamy. Among the Manjas of Ubangi the form can
be seen to change within the same tribe as its members become Chris-
tians. Prior to that, as fetishists, each wife had her own house, and the
man visited a different wife each day, while children also had their own
houses after circumcision. Among the Homboris Moslems of Timbuctoo
each legitimate wife, all concubines, and children above seven have their
own houses, and a rich man's house becomes a vast conglomeration
which is different from an Arab harem of the same size.[45] Among totemic
people exogamy separates men and women even after marriage, and the
Dobu of the Entrecasteaux archipelago have separate dwellings after

[45] Deffontaines, *Géographie et Religions,* p. 20.

marriage, with each village containing five ancestral groups and each couple having two houses, one "patriarchal" and one "matriarchal," and living in them in rotation.[46] Among the Moyombo, men, women, and children all have separate houses, and the complex family organization leads to an extreme breaking up of the house.[47] Among peasants the form of the family also greatly affects house form, as in the case of the Zadrugas in Slavic countries, but enough has been said to show that the basic need of "family," unless much more specifically defined, gives no great insight into house form.

3. POSITION OF WOMEN. While this is an aspect of the family system, it is important enough to merit a few words on its own, and shows the degree of specificity needed in discussing these factors. The Mediterranean area contains two types of houses. There is a two story, stone house with an outside stair found on the coasts and islands from Syria to Catalonia and the Balkans—and in the same area is also the courtyard house.[48] Their occurrence in the same area, and the fact that the court house is very much the same in Greece, North Africa, and Latin America, suggest that the latter relates to some social factor, which may be the extreme need for privacy for women who are cloistered. The windows and roofs of these court houses are designed to prevent anyone from intruding into the intimacy of the house. For the same reason, house doors on opposite sides of the street may not face each other.[49] The outside stair in the other type of house, at least those on Mykonos, is also related to the position of women. On Mykonos the dowry is of great importance, and must include a house; the outside stair enables more than one occupancy in the same house without conflict.

The preeminence of women in the house may take different forms, from the African custom of the man visiting the women's houses and not having one of his own to the subtle distinction between man's and woman's domain in England and America.[50] The position of women may also affect the traditional Japanese house, where the kitchen is one of the few places which is woman's domain and is physically different from the rest of the house. In Egypt men and women are always separated, rich people having separate rooms and poor ones using different corners of their house; this procedure is also followed in the Nomad tent. The dwellings of the Ulufs of Senegal are all turned in their earth enclosure so that houses cannot be seen into from the entry and wives are protected from view.[51] Islamic culture generally affects the form of houses

---

[46] *Ibid.*, p. 113.
[47] *Ibid.*, p. 21.
[48] Sorre, *Fondements de la Géographie Humaine*, pp. 136-137.
[49] Privacy is protected not only by the blank walls, small openings, and other physical devices, but also by custom—few outsiders are ever invited in, and when they are, the women's portion of the house is strictly prohibited.
[50] See E. T. Hall, *The Hidden Dimension* (New York: Doubleday and Co., Inc., 1966), p. 133.
[51] Deffontaines, *Géographie et Religions*, p. 20.

and settlements through the demands of purdah, the harem, and so on, but in each case the specifics of the solution need to be considered.

4. THE NEED FOR PRIVACY. Since privacy is at least partly affected by the position of women, we would expect to find considerable variations in the definition of privacy, how it is achieved, and which are the important considerations.

There are cultures, such as the Sherpas of Nepal, which do not seem to regard privacy as at all essential [52] because of attitudes toward sex; and traditional Japan, before Western influence, had a very different idea of modesty, and hence of privacy. During the summer people would appear naked in public, and used common baths; during the same season one could look right through farmhouses.[53] The Yagua of the Amazon live in a large open house and achieve "privacy" through a social convention which allows someone to become "absent" and, in effect, invisible, by turning away from the center of the house.[54] In addition to attitudes to sex and shame, it is possible that feelings of personal worth, territoriality, and the place of the individual may affect attitudes to privacy. It is the latter factors which may decide whether a communal house is left open and unsubdivided (e.g., the Yagua house or that of the Piaroa Indians of Venezuela) or is divided or even has separate smaller enclosures within it (e.g., the Dyaks and the Kwakiutl).

The desire for privacy may also take forms related to the separation of domains. This can be seen in India, Iran, and Latin America, where the buildings traditionally face inwards (very differently from the outward facing Anglo-American house), and seem independent of the climatic zone or site, occurring in both cities and villages.

In India, each house is surrounded by a low wall or the house elements are arranged around a central court with a blank wall facing the street (Fig. 3.10). It is interesting that in South India, where Moslem influences with regard to purdah are less common, the court is used less frequently and the houses are more open. This pattern, also found in Iran and elsewhere, provides separation of domains and effectively separates the house and its life from both street and neighbors. A clear transition occurs from the noisy public domain to the quiet private one, and from the relatively plain, simple, and restrained exterior to whatever richness and luxury exist inside. There is little concern for what happens in the street, which is merely a way of getting to the fields, wells, or shops, or of defining ethnic and caste groupings. In the traditional settlements, however, the narrow, shady streets become full of life as they

---

[52] C. von Fürer-Heimendorf, *The Sherpas of Nepal,* p. 40.

[53] See Taut, *Houses and People of Japan,* pp. 46, 68 ff., and other writings on traditional Japan. The changes in bathing attitudes due to Western influence, and the lateness of privacy in bathing in the West are significant in considering the "basic" nature of this need.

[54] See Amos Rapoport, "Yagua, or the Amazon Dwelling," *Landscape,* XVI, No. 3 (Spring 1967), 27-30, citing Paul Fejos. I have already referred to the change taking place in Iquitos with the introduction of walls for urban conditions (see figs. 2.1 and 2.2).

FIG. 3.10.   House in northern India.

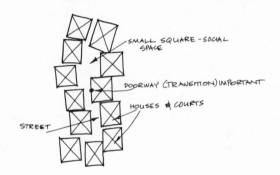

SMALL SQUARE – SOCIAL SPACE

DOORWAY (TRANSITION) IMPORTANT

HOUSES & COURTS

STREET

FIG. 3.11.
Diagrammatic plan of
Punjab village.

serve some social functions. Streets in the Punjab, for example, link the three elements of the village—house, temple or mosque, and bazaar. Widenings in the streets provide room for a small tree or a well, around which a storyteller or small market will set up shop and help the street serve a social function (Fig. 3.11). The transition between street and private domain of the house becomes very important in this case.[55]

[55] See Amos Rapoport, "The Architecture of Isphahan," *Landscape,* XIV, No. 2 (Winter 1964-65), 4-11; Allan B. Jacobs, "Observations on Chandigarh," *AIP Journal,* XXXIII, No. 1 (January 1967), 18 ff. On the neglect of the public realm see David Sopher, "Landscapes and Seasons: Man and Nature in India," *Landscape,* XIII, No. 3 (Spring 1964), 14-19. See also Francis Violich, "Evolution of the Spanish City," *AIP Journal* (August 1962), pp. 170-178, where the distinction is made between the Moslem attitude to the city, with inward facing house and streets as accidental, and the Christian, where the street comes first and houses are outward looking.

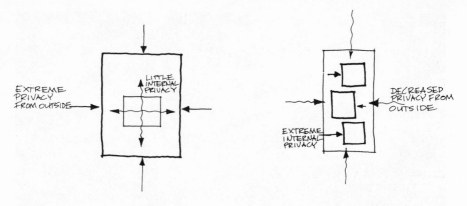

FIG. 3.12. *Privacy realms. Left: Japanese house.*
Right: Western house (Anglo-American).

The Japanese attitude is somewhat similar to India's, although solved differently. The house also turns a blank façade of either walls or high fences to the outside world, and is only open to the street if it has a shop, office, or workshop—all nonresidential uses. Inside the high fence there is little concern with privacy and no worry if people can hear one another and the house can be seen right through. If people stay the night, all sleep next to each other, intermingling both sexes and strangers and householders alike. Privacy depends on the domain (Fig. 3.12). Once again we find a concern with transitions—the entries are not straight, but block views and emphasize the separation of the public and private domains.

This approach of defining privacy in terms of clear separation of domains is also fairly widespread in Africa. An example are the Yoruba of West Africa, who live in mud-walled thatched houses in extended family groups. The houses are usually built in continuous groups of four or more to enclose a square compound reached through a single gateway, not unlike the Kabylie or the houses of India. The outside is a blank expanse of mud wall, with the entry as the only opening, while on the inside, facing the compound, there is a continuous verandah. The clusters of compounds are compactly grouped and form villages or towns with walls around them. The spaces between the compounds form the streets, and there is a space between the compounds and the main walls.[56] Among the Hausa the wall around the compound is the first thing built.

Although architects in our culture often refer to privacy as a basic need, it is really a complex and varied phenomenon.

5. SOCIAL INTERCOURSE. The meeting of people is also a basic need, since man has been defined as a social animal. What concerns us is where

---

[56] These walls are fortified in rather complex manner; defense is important, but the form is not determined by it.

people meet, whether in the house, the cafe, the bath, or the street. This, not the fact of meeting itself, affects the form of the habitat.

The ease with which people can orient themselves in the city is important in helping them socialize, yet the Japanese system is difficult even for the Japanese. In Japan space is organized in a series of *areas* of decreasing size. Within the smallest of these, houses are numbered in the order in which they were built, rather than in the serial order of the Western tradition. Another system of urban orientation, based on street intersections, was imported from China, in early times. This system was never accepted, and neither was the postwar American attempt to name streets in Tokyo.

After one has found one's way about, the specific *how* and *where* of the meeting are important. In the Chinese village people meet in the wide part of the main street; in North Africa it may be the well for women and the cafe for men; in the Bantu village it is the space between the animal pens and the walls of the living compound. In Chan Kom in Yucatán the meeting place is the steps of the little village store, while in Turkey and Malaya it is the coffee shop. In France it used to be the cafe and *bistro,* and guests were never invited into the house. This procedure is now changing, and the house is used more, affecting both house form and the city. In Italy it is the piazza, galleria, and cafe, in England the pub and house. Some areas, such as San Luis, Guatemala, Dragoe, Denmark, and many parts of Greece, have periodic promenades or gatherings during which the social area expands over a larger area than normally used. This is a temporal rather than spatial solution, although it actually involves both, and becomes an important and complex aspect of the urban setting.

The Relation of House and Settlement

The discussion dealing with separation of domains and social intercourse suggests that the house cannot be seen in isolation from the settlement, but must be viewed as part of a total social and spatial system which relates the house, way of life, settlement, and even landscape. Man lives in the whole settlement of which the house is only a part, and the way in which he uses the settlement affects house form, as, for example, in areas where the meeting place is the house, and others where the meeting place is a part of the settlement, such as a street or plaza. Geography as well as architecture has usually separated study of the house from that of settlement, yet the need to look at the house as part of a larger system confirms that the house conveys little sense outside of its setting and context. Because the living pattern always extends beyond the house to some degree, the form of the house is affected by the extent to which one lives in it and the range of activities that take place in it. For example, the fact that many peasants in Latin America and other developing countries only use the house as a place in which to sleep, store things, and corral animals, and most living takes place outside has far-reaching implications for house form. Although this discussion brings us close to the topic of urban design, which is outside the compass of this book, we must get involved in it to understand the extent to which the settlement pattern affects the house.

There have been many types of classifications proposed for settlements, and most writers have commented on the difficulty of definition and the fact that most forms are not pure but mixed. The common classification into dispersed and concentrated settlements will undoubtedly affect house form because activities which need to take place in the house in the dispersed case could, possibly, occur within the settlement in the concentrated case. But even in the concentrated settlement a distinction, which is of great importance to the understanding of the relation of settlement and dwelling and its effect on house form, needs to be made.

There have generally been two traditions of concentrated settlement. In one the whole settlement has been considered as the setting for life, and the dwelling merely as a more private, enclosed, and sheltered part of the living realm. In the other the dwelling has essentially been regarded as the total setting for life, and the settlement, whether village or city, as connective tissue, almost "waste" space to be traversed, and secondary in nature. This distinction is stated here in extreme form and is greatly simplified. Between the two types described is a whole range with differing amounts of use of the outside space—but the general distinction does hold.[57] (Diagrammatically the two patterns may be represented as in Fig. 3.13.)

In Western culture we may consider the Latin, Mediterranean village or town as typical of the first type, and the Anglo-American city as typical of the second, with Los Angeles as an extreme example where only the private realm, the house and backyard, is really used (not considering the use of parks and beaches as using the *city*). Within the context of a given culture, we may regard the vernacular tradition as typical of the first, and the grand design tradition as typical of the second.

This distinction between types may be due partly to written or unwritten laws which limit the behavior patterns in the different domains— public or private—by prohibiting some and allowing others. This is an expression of world view and other attitudes, and is one way in which a culture is linked to the way people use space.[58] In the same way the distinction may be due partly to the effect of religion on social attitudes and family, and hence on the separation of domains.

This distinction is fundamental and applies to prehistoric, primitive, and non-European examples as much as to our own culture. In the early Iron Age we can compare the scattered single family farmsteads of England, as at Little Woodbury, Wiltshire, with the highly organized settlements of the continent, or the lakeside settlements of Scotland and Ireland, where the settlement *is* the house.

Among primitive people we can find almost every possible type along

---

[57] This concept was initially Robert Cresswell's in "Les Concepts de la Maison: Les Peuples non Industriels," *Zodiac* 7 (1960), pp. 182-197. Since then I have modified and elaborated it.

[58] For example, see the discussion in Erving Goffman, *Behavior in Public Places* (New York: Free Press, 1963), pp. 56-59.

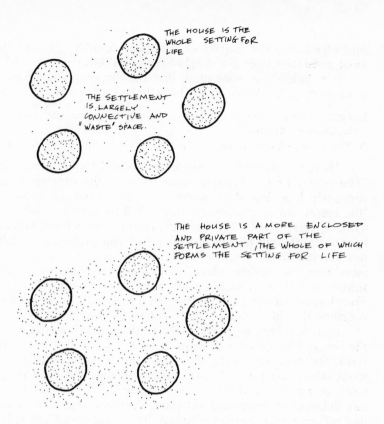

FIG. 3.13.   The two house-settlement systems.

the scale, from the Lodi of West Africa, who have little communal life and whose houses stand by themselves and form the total setting for life, to the Cayapa of Ecuador, who use their villages only for festivals and whose house is the settlement, and the Aymara of the Andean plateau, whose setting for life is the whole settlement, the house being used only at night.

The Aymara pattern is almost "African," because it is generally among the primitive people of Africa that the creation of the larger "place" for living is very common, although not universal. In the Kabylie the house is also just a small part of the larger realm and represents its *private* portion, and the same applies to New Guinea, where the dance ground and men's ceremonial house are much more important than the dwelling house.

It could be argued that the manner in which the settlement is used will depend on the climate, and it is obvious that the climate will play a role—but, as usual, this is not the whole story. The Aymara of the Altiplano live in a very harsh and cold climate. The city as a whole is used in Paris in the winter, although the situation is changing as cafes become less popular. Australia and California, while very outdoor minded in their use of beaches, parks, and sports facilities, hardly ever use the

71

settlement or town. It is interesting that the situation is changing in Australia under the impact of European immigrants, and that there is great resistance from the Anglo-Saxon establishment.

It is indeed my contention that the distinction between uses of the settlement, in the Western world, is linked culturally in these two ways:

1. Latin, Mediterranean cultures vs. Anglo-American cultures (as one contemporary example).
2. The vernacular tradition vs. the high style tradition within a given culture.

There is a perceptive comment by Karel Capek regarding England: "The poetry of the English home exists at the expense of the English street which is devoid of poetry" and that street has been described as "the empty street, the lonely street." [59] This does not fully apply to the working class streets, i.e., the more vernacular setting, where the street is used,[60] although far less than it is in Latin countries. A similar distinction is found in the way the American working class uses the street much more than the middle class.[61] The simple dichotomy is obviously too simple, and there is such a wide range of ways of using the city that a Frenchman can compare the French and Brazilian use of the street and conclude that his countrymen do not really use the street! [62]

It is clear that the form of the settlement affects the way of life and the house. The Zapotec of Oaxaca display three different settlement patterns—the compact town, the semicompact town, and the semivacant town, where the center is used for ceremonies and most people live and work in *ranchos* and have two households.[63] Each of the settlements has different customs and behavior, different attitudes to many things, and different man-woman relations. These variations are reflected in the houses, their forms, and space allocations in them, even if direct causal relations cannot be traced.

The settlement pattern can also affect attitudes to innovation, as in the cases of the Navajo and Zuñi. When veterans came back after World War II the Navajo, who have a dispersed living pattern, were able to accept innovation because it affected only the single household and did not disrupt the community. Among the Zuñi, whose settlement pattern is compact, any innovation would have affected the whole community and was resisted.[64]

59 Čapek cited in Walter Creese, *The Search for Environment* (New Haven: Yale University Press, 1966), p. 105. The other comment is on p. 82.
60 See Reyner Banham, *The New Brutalism* (London: The Architectural Press, 1966), p. 42.
61 See the work of Marc Fried on the West End of Boston, e.g., "Grieving for a Lost Home," in Leonard Duhl, *The Urban Condition* (New York and London: Basic Books, 1963), pp. 151-171, esp. pp. 153, 155-157.
62 See Lévi-Strauss, *Tristes Tropiques*, p. 57. In the American tradition see the report of the 1811 Manhattan Plan Commissioners, cited in Tunnard and Reed, *American Skyline* (New York: Houghton Mifflin, 1956), p. 57, from which it is obvious that the city is only thought of as a set of houses and has no independent existence.
63 Laura Nader, *Talea and Juquila* (a comparison of Zapotec social organization), University of California Publications in American Anthropology and Ethnology, XLVIII, No. 3, 1964, and personal communications.
64 Professor Laura Nader, Department of Anthropology, University of California, Berkeley, personal communication.

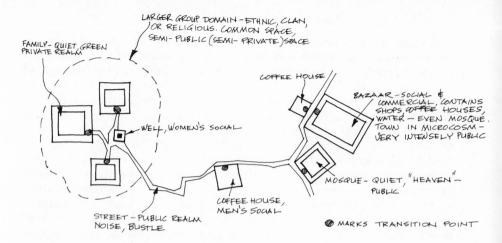

FIG. 3.14. *Diagram of house-settlement system in Moslem town (Isphahan). Shows some of the activities only.*

Houses, settlements, and landscapes are products of the same cultural system and world view, and are therefore parts of a single system. In traditional Japan, for example, the separation of domains results in each house being isolated and each household doing what it wishes; as long as common values are shared, variations in house form within an order produce good results. Once the shared values disappear or are weakened, the same attitudes produce the visual chaos of the Japanese city today. No one takes responsibility for the public area because it is little used as part of the total living realm. The Japanese word for town is the same as that for street.[65] Since the city was never meant to be used by the citizens,[66] it, and its houses, are regarded very differently than they are in the West.

It is, therefore, important to see the house not only in relation to the basic dichotomy of settlement types as settings for life and their variants along the total space-use scale, but also as part of the specific system to which it belongs. It needs to be viewed in relation to the town, its monumental parts, nondomestic areas, and social meeting places, and the way they and the urban spaces are used—we need only think of the different ways in which the dwelling is used in Paris and in Los Angeles for this need to become clear. In addition, we must consider the movement from the house, through the various transitions to the street, and then to the other parts of the settlement (Fig. 3.14).

[65] Taut, *Houses and People of Japan,* p. 226.
[66] Eiyo Ishikawa, *The Study of Shopping Centers in Japanese Cities and Treatment of Reconstructing,* Memoirs of the faculty of Science and Engineering No. 17 (Tokyo: Waseda University, 1953). The author points out that the Japanese city never had squares or other public spaces as did the European city, and that community life has had to take place in different ways, beginning with pleasure resorts and then amusement centers.

The Site and Its Choice

There are two ways in which the effect of the site on buildings can be considered. The first would deal with the physical nature of the site—its slope, type of rock or soil, run-off, vegetative cover, microclimate, and so on; the second would consider the symbolic, religious, or cultural values of the site and their consequences. While the physical nature of the site does affect building form, as in the case of a steeply sloping site, it is the initial choice of site that introduces this variable. In this choice access to food or water, exposure to wind, defensive potential, the sparing of land for agriculture, and transportation all play a role. Defense may lead to the choice of a high point in the curve of a river, the shore of a lake, or a steep hill. For trade the presence of a ford may be a consideration, and for transportation in a jungle the bank of a river may be important. In the final analysis, choice of site depends largely on socio-cultural values, which helps explain why the Meo in Southeast Asia pick hills for their houses, while the Man, with a similar setting and economy, pick flat areas. While the need to preserve arable land plays a role in the siting of the Peruvian *marca,* the houses of New Caledonia, or the pueblos, the latter are found on both the plains and mesa tops, their siting related to the six cardinal points and the sacred directions of North and East.

Siting, and to a degree building form, are mainly the result of social factors, which may include family or clan structure and grouping; relation to animals, and the spatial relations with them, as with the Masai; relation to grain, as in the Cameroons and the Pueblos; attitudes to nature; the needs of magic and sacred orientation; and the symbolism of landscape features. The choice of what is regarded as a good site brings with it physical effects and some consequent adjustments. The influence of physical effects on the siting of buildings and hence on their forms and relations can be strong. The novelist Karen Blixen (Isak Dinesen), in *Out of Africa,* described her attempts to lay out grids for African workers' houses on her ranch, their refusal to follow these grids, and their fitting of their houses into the site after study of the configuration of the land, hills, hollows, rocks, and creeks. But it is the cultural aspects of the choice of site that seem most crucial, and on which I will concentrate.

The fact that sites are chosen on the basis of myth, religion, and way of life rather than on utilitarian or physical grounds has been pointed out by a number of writers. For example, consideration of mountains as "good" or "bad" involves a choice of this nature. In the same area of the Verde valley in New Mexico, the Hohokam (A.D. 700-1100) built on the flat or on terraces, while the Sinagua (A.D. 1100-1400) built on the hills and mesas. Even when terraces were left vacant by the Hohokam, the Sinagua never built on them.[67]

Decisions are made in the same way as to whether one builds on river banks or avoids them, or uses the desert, as the Bedouin do, or avoids it.

[67] See A. H. Shroeder, "Man and Environment in the Verde Valley," *Landscape,* III, No. 2 (Winter 1953-1954), 17-18. Originally, of course, the high ground might have been preferred because it was above malarial swamps or because of winds, but eventually it became traditional, characteristic of the culture, and used in different contexts.

Such decisions express in large measure the feeling of desirability of site based on nonutilitarian grounds. An extreme example is the big island of Malekula in the New Hebrides, where residence is prohibited: the people live on small islands around it and have to travel to the large island for cultivation and even water. On the small islands themselves the village pattern, location of houses, and choice of site depend on extremely complex religious attitudes.[68]

All this suggests that the attitude toward nature and site would be an important aspect of the creation of house form, or its modification by the site, and that the relation of man to landscape is the first aspect which needs to be considered. A number of classifications of such attitudes have been proposed, but the most useful from our point of view examines it in terms of the I–Thou and I–It relation, which historically takes three forms:

1. *Religious and cosmological.* The environment is regarded as dominant, and man is less than nature.
2. *Symbiotic.* Here man and nature are in a state of balance, and man regards himself as responsible to God for nature and the earth and as a steward and custodian of nature.[69]
3. *Exploitative.* Man is the completer and modifier of nature, then creator, and finally destroyer of the environment.

In the first two forms nature and the landscape are a *Thou*, the relation is personal, and nature is to be worked *with*, while in the third nature is an *It* to be worked *on*, exploited, and used. This form indicates a basic change no matter when it occurs—chronology does not affect the basic argument.[70]

As I have pointed out, the effects of primitive man on the landscape are minimal, particularly as far as the individual is concerned. For primitive man and, to a lesser extent, peasant people, the relation of man with nature, and hence with landscape and site, is personal; there is no sharp distinction between man and nature.[71] The primary world view is of harmony with nature rather than of conflict or conquest; the concept of man/not man in primitive societies is above all one of mutuality—man

---

[68] Deffontaines, *Géographie et Religions,* pp. 115-116. On p. 148 he makes the general point that "the founder chooses the location not from geographical conditions but by seeking to conform to the decisions of the gods" (my translation). While he is referring to cities, it also applies to the house and even to its parts, as we have seen.

[69] J. B. Jackson in a lecture at the University of California, Berkeley, October 30, 1962, suggested that this view is still prevalent in Calvinist Switzerland and explains the careful use of the landscape in that country.

[70] Redfield, *The Primitive World,* p. 110, suggests that this change is post-Cartesian; C. Glacken, *Traces on the Rhodian Shore* (Los Angeles and Berkeley: University of California Press, 1967), suggests that these three attitudes have coexisted in the high cultures from the earliest times. The view that nature is inanimate matter which is to be exploited by applying technology for man's comfort, and that this is man's aim, reaches the ultimate in the United States, the Soviet Union, Australia, and so on.

[71] Robert Redfield, *The Primitive World,* pp. 9, 11, 105; *Peasant Society and Culture,* pp. 112 ff.; Birket-Smith, *Primitive Man and His Ways,* p. 23.

is in nature and one cannot speak of man *and* nature.[72] This view and the consequent relation of man and animals result in attitudes toward differentiation and specialization which I have discussed in relation to both work and space, and affect siting in both primitive and preindustrial cultures.

This attitude has an effect on the form of both the settlement and the house. For example, it has been suggested that the pueblos are greatly affected by their site, and that their rooms, which are caves, are joined together to be like a mesa. The pueblo looks like a land form because the close relation of house form and landscape reflects the harmony of man and nature. The whole landscape is sacred, as is the house, and the whole environment influences all of Pueblo life.[73] In fact, Pueblo Indians beg forgiveness every time they fell a tree or kill a jack rabbit. Corn growing is for them a religious act and an essential part of the total spiritual life. It is this attitude which affects the house, its form, siting, and relation to the land, and helps explain why such buildings enhance rather than damage the landscape.

The Maya pray when they clear the forest, and the maize field is sacred; the Pygmies feel that if they upset the balance of nature they have to restore it, and perform ceremonies when they kill an animal or fell a tree, very much like the Pueblo Indians, and for a similar reason —the belief that there is a spiritual harmony between man and nature. Among some primitive people, anyone who leaves his native region is treated as dead and receives funeral rites; exile is equivalent to a death sentence. This is, of course, due to identification of the land with the social group through its ancestors, an identification well expressed in African "ritual" whereby a native who brings back a wife from another region carries to her some earth from his area. "Every day she has to eat a bit of this dirt . . . to accustom herself to this change of residence." [74]

This general attitude of respect and reverence for the site means that one does not browbeat or rape it (or nature in general) but works with the site. Buildings fit into the landscape and express this attitude through choice of siting, materials, and forms. These forms not only satisfy cultural, symbolic, and utilitarian requirements, but often are so much a part of the site that it cannot be imagined without the dwelling, village, or town. Such qualities also reflect the presence of shared goals and values, a clear and agreed-on purpose, and an accepted hierarchical structure of house, settlement, and landscape, as well as direct response to climate and technology. The forms are also a clear reflection of needs, leading to the direct and intuitively clear feeling of rightness described above. A description of how this can affect a sensitive observer is to be found in the opening paragraphs of Adolf Loos' *Architektur*. He describes

---

[72] Redfield, *The Primitive World*, p. 105; on p. 106, he refers to man and nature being bound together in one moral order, and on p. 107 states that the whole universe is morally significant.

[73] See Paul Horgan, "Place, Form and Prayer," *Landscape*, III, No. 2 (Winter 1953-54), pp. 8-9.

[74] Lucien Lévy-Bruhl, *Primitive Mentality*, trans. Lilian A. Clare (Boston: Beacon Press, 1966), p. 214. See also Birket-Smith, *Primitive Man and His Ways*, p. 28, discussing the strong religious ties that bind Australian aborigines to the land. If this link with the land is cut the tribe may disintegrate.

the shores of a mountain lake, commending the homogeneity of everything in the scene, including the houses of the peasants. All seems "shaped by the hand of God," and then

. . . here, what is this? A false note, a scream out of place. Among the houses of the peasants, which were made not by them but by God, stands a villa. Is it the work of a good architect or a bad one? I don't know. I only know that the peace and the beauty of the scene have been ruined . . . how is it that every architect, good or bad, causes harm to the lake? The peasant does not do this.[75]

My answer has already been implied. Unselfconsciousness, lack of pretension or desire to impress, direct response to way of life, climate, and technology, use of the "model and variations" method of building, attitude toward nature and landscape, all play a part. The latter affects the relation of built form to land form, the making of *places*, and consequently affects the building form itself. I am able here to discuss only one aspect of this matter, using the African village as an example.

Comparison of traditional villages with the new townships in Africa has concerned many architects and planners. While the higher physical standards of the new townships are acknowledged, so is their "deadly dullness." On that point two points of view can be found. The first generally disparages the indigenous villages, attributing the dullness of the new townships to the need for economy (although the traditional villages are at a lower economic level) and to their being one story (although so are the native villages). Solutions proposed involve a series of such cosmetic devices as colors, planting, and vertical features which ignore the basic differences between the two types of settlements. The other, more thoughtful, view compares the new townships less favorably with the traditional villages, not just visually but functionally—although it is clear that the two aspects cannot be separated, and both are linked to the relation with the land.

The charm and vitality of the traditional forms and the drabness, dullness, and monotony of the new ones, designed by architects, is due to more than the charm of the picturesque. The unity of plan, site, and materials in traditional villages generates an enthusiastic response even in most lay observers. Much of this response is evoked by harmony with the landscape, as well as a feeling of fitness to purpose, directness, and forcefulness. An intimate scale is created by a series of walls which not only enclose space, but also tie the houses together and link them to the landscape. The horizontality of the flat walls is contrasted with the verticality of the cylindrical houses and conical roofs, a contrast not only of enclosure and form but also of colors and textures of materials—earth, grass, thatch, timber, and stone—which accentuate differences but are all related to the landscape. The houses are related to the landscape through the strong geometry, some never using a straight line.[76] The flowing lines of the

---

[75] Quoted in Reyner Banham, *Theory and Design in the First Machine Age* (New York: Frederick A. Praeger, Inc., 1960), pp. 96-97.

[76] Some of these cultures do not have a word for straight, and are not susceptible to the various optical illusions based on straight lines and used in experimental perception work. See R. L. Gregory, *Eye and Brain* (New York: McGraw-Hill Book Company, 1966), p. 161, and M. H. Segall *et al.*, *The Influence of Culture on Visual Perception* (Indianapolis: Bobbs-Merrill, Inc., 1966), pp. 66; 186.

buildings sit on the natural contours, showing a flair for visually combining and relating groups of buildings with such natural features as rock outcrops, trees, and land forms. The quality of these buildings is due as much to their being an expression of group consciousness as to the blending of building and land into a whole.

In the new townships the grid destroys both the intimate scale and the link with the land. The new visual elements no longer express the relation of the individual to the group and of the group to the land as the larger living realm does in the traditional pattern. The new pattern makes the individual feel insignificant. Group unity is destroyed, and there is no clear relation of man to his surroundings through elements of increasing spatial scale and demarcation of domains in harmony with the land around.[77]

Constancy and Change [78]

Attaching so much importance to the culturally linked aspects of built form tends to lead to a position of complete relativism. As soon as a given culture or way of life has changed, its form would become meaningless. Yet we know that many artifacts retain validity when the culture which created them has long since disappeared, and that housing and settlement forms are still usable, even though the meaning attached to the forms may have changed very greatly. In fact, in human, as opposed to technological, terms, such forms may often be superior. For example, the Mexican house and the settlement pattern of which it forms part is superior to the American house in many ways, and the European medieval town is more liveable, and satisfies many perceptual needs better, than contemporary towns. This suggests that certain aspects of behavior and the way of life are constant, or change very slowly, and that replacement of old forms is often due to the prestige value of novelty rather than lack of utility or even unsatisfactory relation to the way of life. Similarly, of course, acceptance of old forms may also be due to the prestige value of old things rather than any real continued validity or utility of the forms. In either case, although both attitudes to old forms are culturally linked, an element of constancy which needs to be further explored seems to be involved, or at least possible.

It may be suggested that the nature of man and his institutions contains elements of both constancy and change which affect the subject of built form and can be considered in relation to the biological nature of man, his perception, and his behavior.

The evidence with regard to man's biological nature is much more strongly in favor of constancy than is the case for perception and behavior.

[77] See paper by P. H. Connel, presented at the Fourth Congress of South African Architects and Quantity Surveyors, Durham, May 1947. See also Balandier, *Afrique Ambiguë*, pp. 202-203, 206 ff., 213, 224-226.
[78] The term is Siegfried Giedion's; see *The Eternal Present* (New York: Pantheon Books, 1962, 1964). René Dubos, *Man Adapting*, refers to permanency and change. My use of the terms is rather different, however. This whole section is particularly speculative and, while explored at a graduate seminar at the University of California, Berkeley, is far from complete.

It seems clear that man has changed little in body and physiology since his beginnings.[79] If man does, in fact, have certain inborn rhythms, biological needs, and responses which are unchanging, a complete relativism becomes impossible and the built environment of the past may still be valid. If this also applies to emotional needs and responses, and to patterns of behavior, then it will have a major impact on the interpretation of built form and its significance.

There is some evidence both for the view that *perception* and *behavior* are culturally linked, and therefore changeable, and for the view that they are inborn and hence constant. Existence of two possible points of view is, in itself, significant in view of our culture's prevailing stress on the element of change in man and his buildings. It would seem that, in general, the elements of change are more dominant than those of constancy, as we would expect from the cultural basis of built form which I have proposed. However, rather than try to decide in favor of either one or the other, it may be suggested that there are *both* constant and changeable elements. We can say that there are certain constant factors which do not change, and which may have high criticality, but that the specific forms these needs take are culturally linked and changeable—and of lower criticality.

For example, the need for sensory stimulation and satisfaction, and hence for visual and social complexity in the environment, seems constant for both man and animals,[80] but the specific forms that provide for these needs may be different. The psychological need for *security*, expressed by shelter, may be constant, while its specific expression in building may vary greatly; the same applies to the religious and ceremonial impulse. The need for communication is constant, while the specific symbols vary.[81]

The consequences of this coexistence of elements for the understanding of built form may become clearer if we consider one example at greater length. We may regard the territorial instinct, the need for *identity*, and "place," as constant and essential, and therefore of high criticality, while regarding its various manifestations as culturally linked. Although this results in different ways in which territory and the ideal environment are defined, the situation is still very different than it would be if we regarded the instinct as not present in man, since one of the basic functions of the house may be the definition of territory. Thus the distinction between what is constant and what is changeable may be helpful in understanding the form and motivations of both houses and settlements.

The distinction between constant and changeable aspects may have profound consequences on the house and the city. The distinction among the different types of urban space made by some French urban sociologists

[79] See Dubos, *Man Adapting.*
[80] See Amos Rapoport and Robert E. Kantor, "Complexity and Ambiguity in Environmental Design," *Journal of the AIP*, XXXIII, No. 4 (July 1967), 210-221. This need has recently been shown to apply even to organisms as primitive as the planarium.
[81] An analogous argument in another, although related, field is Carl Jung's work with symbolism—the tendency to plan symbols is constant, but the forms, the images, vary. See Jung, *Man and His Symbols* (Garden City, N.Y.: Doubleday and Co., 1964), pp. 66 ff. Also see pp. 24, 47, on primitive man, and p. 52, pointing out that these primitive layers are still with us.

—physical space, economic space, social space, and many others—can be partly understood in these terms, while architects have suggested that one can usefully distinguish between technological space, such as bathrooms and service spaces, which is changing as equipment and services change, and symbolic, largely living, space, which is constant and usable almost indefinitely. This latter type of space is related to territoriality and clarifies the concepts of "ethnic domain," separation of spaces inside the house or tent, and separation of domains. The concept of the ethnic domain and the definition of place is fundamental.[82] The specific definition of place is variable—one man's place may be another man's nonplace, and the definition of the good life, and consequently the setting for it, also vary greatly. Since *how* things are done may be more important than *what* is done, the element of change is dominant in varying degrees, but not to the exclusion of constancy, as is commonly assumed.

The sanctity of the threshold is also probably related to this constant need to define territory, but the specific manner in which it is defined varies in different cultures and periods, and constitutes the element of change. Not only do devices for defining threshold vary, but the threshold itself occurs at different points in the total space. The compound in India, or the Mexican or Moslem house, put the threshold further forward than the Western house does, and the fence of the English house puts it further forward than the open lawn of the American suburb (Fig. 3.15). In each case, however, the threshold separating the two domains is present.

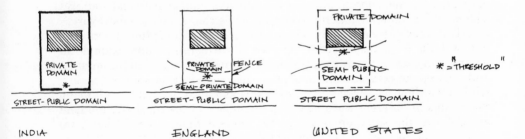

FIG. 3.15. *Approximate location of "threshold" in three cultures.*

One could ask whether the definition of territory, which seems basic to the house, makes life easier by giving cues for behavior (the house as a social mechanism), and whether people, like animals, feel more secure and better able to defend themselves on their home ground.[83] This need for security may be one of the reasons why man has to define place, and

[82] People in office buildings react very strongly to having to give up a space which they have made theirs, and there has been resistance to buildings where personalization of space—territorializing—is impossible. See Amos Rapoport, "Whose Meaning in Architecture," *Arena*, LXXXIII, No. 916; and *Interbuild*, XIV, No. 10 (London, October 1967), 44-46.
[83] As we have seen, this definition may be symbolic, as in the case of some American Indians whose meeting houses are secret but physically *open*.

Anglo-Saxon law, as well as other legal systems, recognizes this by protecting the home from intrusion, even permitting killing in its defense.

Another aspect of territoriality is *crowding*. The recent work of such ethologists as Calhoun and Christian, and the work of Chombart de Lauwe, has suggested that man, no less than animals, is subject to the stresses generated by penetration of the individual's "bubble" of space. Man is better able to deal with these stresses than, for example, rats, since his defenses are more effective. Man's social defense mechanisms seem more constant than his physical mechanisms and specific devices, which are more changeable and culturally defined. In fact, the ability to deal with the problem of crowding varies with the culture, and we may consider the house and the settlement as more or less successful devices for dealing with it.[84] The Japanese Inn serves as a device for relieving tension, and the Japanese house may also be such a device. This would help to account for Japanese resistance to shared walls, the use of entry "locks" similar to the ones in Isphahan and other Moslem areas, and the garden and tea house.[85] It may be said that such devices become more strongly marked as one considers dwellings along a scale of increasing crowding; attitudes to noise and privacy may also vary, since they are social defense mechanisms.

Courtyard houses, and separation of domains in general, are used in cultures which are *both crowded and hierarchic*, and the prevalence of such houses in all their manifestations, from the simple house of Jericho, through those of Greece, Rome, Islam, India, and Latin America, to the very complex *Jen* house of China, with its many courts, may be due to a similar need (Fig. 3.16). The principle behind them is the same, and their form remains similar over long periods and large areas. The need is to get away while still in the familiar territory of the family or clan group —and the separation of domains achieves that. In cultures with no over-all hierarchy this type of development does not take place. An awareness of all these factors—the constancy of the need, the territorial instinct, and the relation of house to settlement—helps our understanding of built form.

The value of past solutions is another instance of constancy, since solutions proposed as novel are often identical to those used in traditional cultures for millennia.[86]

In summary, it could be said that the form determinants of the house can be divided into constant and changeable ones, and that the whole problem of constancy and change can be related to built form in this way for a number of variables. I have already referred to the great stability of forms and the fact that we can still use old forms with considerable

---

[84] See Chap. 6 on the differences among the abilities of people such as Italians, Germans, and Americans to deal with noise and other consequences of crowding.

[85] The widespread use of entertainment and amusement areas in Japanese cities may have a similar function.

[86] The use of the "half-way house" in the work on urban forms for India by Prof. Richard Meier, University of Michigan, recalls the use of such devices in primitive cultures, as in the Bororo village described by Lévi-Strauss, and the natural staged migrations of the Peruvians from the Altiplano to the city. Other examples of constancy are the prevalence of ethnic enclaves in cities still found in India and Moslem countries, which has also had to be considered in recent housing in Israel.

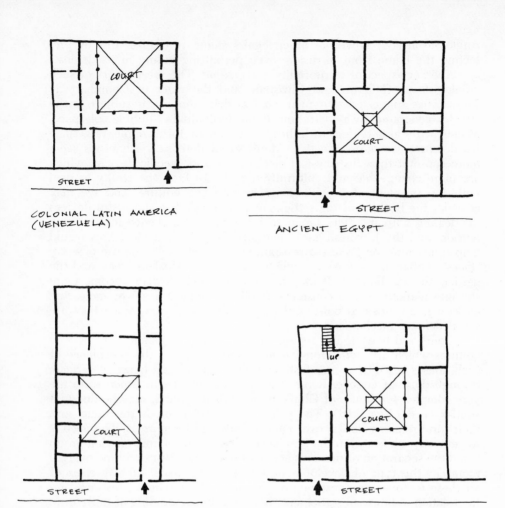

FIG. 3.16. *Four courtyard houses. Houses of similar* principle
can be found in Rome, China, Spain, Ur,
Babylon, Islamic countries, and many other areas.

success. A Pueblo Indian could live in a building of 600 years ago,[87]
and I have myself lived in such old houses more comfortably than in
more recent ones. In fact, I would suggest that anyone could live in an
ancient Greek house, for example, with the only needed adjustment being
to the technological spaces.

[87] J. B. Jackson, "Pueblo Architecture and Our Own," *Landscape,* III, No. 2 (Winter
1953-54), 17. See also Amos Rapoport, "Yagua, or the Amazon Dwelling"; Edgar
Anderson, "The City Is a Garden," *Landscape,* VII, No. 2 (Winter 1957-58), 5,
on the comfort and advantages of the old house in Mexico and its validity as a
form.

CHAPTER 4 *climate as a* *modifying factor*

While I have suggested that climatic determinism fails to account for the range and diversity of house forms, climate is, nevertheless, an important aspect of the form-generating forces, and has major effects on the forms man may wish to create for himself. This is to be expected under conditions of weak technology and limited environmental control systems, where man cannot dominate nature but must adapt to it.

The impact of the climatic factor will depend on its severity and forcefulness, hence the degree of freedom it allows; I have suggested the usefulness of the climatic scale. I will discuss this concept further, although it is obvious that a South Sea islander has more choices than an Eskimo even though the latter has some choice.

The principal aspect to be examined is the amazing skill shown by primitive and peasant builders in dealing with climatic problems, and their ability to use minimum resources for maximum comfort. (For the purposes of this chapter the anticlimatic solutions already referred to will be largely neglected.) One is repeatedly struck by the knowledge and discrimination of such builders in selection of sites and materials suitable to the specific local microclimate, and, in the case of peasant builders, in adapting the traditional model to these conditions. The traditional requirements for siting and form which may sometimes have a climatic rationale often become too rigid, not allowing for adjustments of the model for specific local requirements, even in peasant cultures.

E. B. White wrote:

I am pessimistic about the human race because it is too clever for its own good. Our approach to nature is to beat it into submission. We would stand a better chance for survival if we accommodated ourselves to this planet and viewed it appreciatively instead of skeptically and dictatorially.[1]

---

[1] Quoted with Mr. White's permission.

While this is meant to apply to man's action on other living things and resources, it is also relevant to his dealings with climate through the use of buildings. For the purpose of this chapter, buildings may be regarded as thermal control devices—with the usual proviso about the danger of isolating single variables.

The commonly expressed view that there is no area in the United States which does not require air-conditioning indicates that we tend to ignore the climate. Our modern solutions to climatic problems often do not work, and our houses are made bearable by means of ingenious mechanical devices whose cost sometimes exceeds that of the building shell. The comfort created by these devices is still problematical, and may lead to such unforeseen dangers as an overcontrolled and uniform environment; man may not be so much controlling the environment as escaping it.[2] The poor thermal performance of many of our buildings despite this mass of mechanical equipment suggests that we cannot ignore the physical environment, and that we underestimate its continued effect on our cities and buildings.

Primitive and preindustrial builders cannot take this attitude, since they lack the technology to allow them to ignore climate in design. In light of their attitude to nature, it is doubtful that they would use such tools even if they were available to them. Therefore, primitive, and to a lesser extent peasant, builders are faced with the task of creating shelter for a wide range of climatic conditions. For their own comfort (and occasionally even survival), they have to create, with very limited materials and technology, buildings which respond successfully to the climate. It could be argued that, if we consider hostility of environment and available resources, the problems faced by the Eskimo are not unlike those involved in the design of a space capsule. The difference is less than one would imagine.

These builders and craftsmen have learned to solve their problems by collaborating with nature. Since any failure would mean having to face the harsh forces of nature personally—which is not the case with an architect designing for someone else—their buildings have largely been designed as natural shells to protect and help the way of life, *no matter what that might be*. Louis Kahn remarked after coming back from Africa:

I saw many huts that the natives made. They were all alike, and they all worked. There were no architects there. I came back with impressions of how clever was man who solved the problems of sun, rain, wind.[3]

Primitive man often builds more wisely than we do, and follows principles of design which we ignore at great cost. We must not romanticize his accomplishments, however. With respect to many of our standards of size, amenity, safety, and permanence, the actual forms of many of his buildings are totally unsuitable, and it has been pointed out re-

---

[2] René Dubos, *Man Adapting* (New Haven: Yale University Press, 1966), pp. 14, 28, 42 ff., 51, 55, 88, 422-423, and elsewhere in this very important book.
[3] "A Statement by Louis Kahn," *Arts and Architecture*, LXXVIII, No. 2 (February 1961), 29.

peatedly how unhealthy and unhygienic such buildings may be.[4] The
principles, and in some cases the actual accomplishments, are of value;
in any event, such attempts to solve the problems of climate must have
important form consequences.

The Climatic Scale

Man was faced with the problem of designing for climate as soon as
he left those areas where no shelter from climate was needed, and left
the shelter of the cave in less hospitable areas. In these terms, the house
is a container whose main purpose is to shelter and protect its occupants
and contents from animal and human enemies and those natural forces
known as *the weather.* It is a tool which frees man for other activities
by creating an environment which suits him, protecting him from the
undesirable effects of his surroundings.

The need for shelter varies with the severity of the forces to be
overcome, and the climatic scale is a useful concept for determining the
need. This scale, if drawn, would range from need for no shelter at all,
on *climatic* grounds alone, to areas with a maximum need for shelter.
The solutions in each case will provide the maximum amount of protection
in terms of the given technological resources and the socially defined
needs. The more severe the climatic constraints, the more will the form
be limited and fixed, and less variation will be possible from what one
could term "pure climatic functionalism"; hence, less choice will be possible. However, the criticality never limits choice entirely. Although the
cold winters in mountain areas mean that people and animals must
spend almost all their time indoors, the specific form of the shelter is
still open to considerable choice.

We would expect to find the most forceful, enlightening solutions
in those areas where climate is most severe and physical environment
most difficult. Traditionally, the most common examples have been the
Arctic, especially the superb Igloo of the North American Arctic; the
desert, particularly the mud and stone houses of the desert belts of the
Old and New Worlds; and the humid tropics, with their classical solution
of raised floor, wide eaves, and no walls. Indeed it is essential that these
be considered, but possibly in a wider context. A greater number of
examples is needed to show the deliberate nature of the solutions, the
awareness of the need and the response, and the existence of anticlimatic
solutions.

Builders under difficult conditions do show a detailed knowledge
of the forms, materials, and micro-climate of the area. They know the

---

[4] See Max Sorre, *Les Fondements de la Géographie Humaine,* Vol. 3 (Paris: Armand
Colin, 1952), pp. 147-148; see also a recent study at the University of Melbourne
which has shown that, in New Guinea, dirt dropping down from thatched roofs
results in chronic allergic lung diseases (*The New York Times,* July 16, 1967,
p. 55). In Venezuela the thatch and wattle and daub construction often harbors
insects which carry an endemic disease (Chagas). There is also some evidence of
Eskimo dwellings leading to bronchiectasis, a pulmonary complaint. See *The New
York Times,* August 9, 1967, p. 23.

FIG. 4.1. *Development of Australian house from ca. 1840 to ca. 1884.*

absorbent, reflective, and other characteristics of local materials for maximum comfort and their resistance to rain and snow. The accurate knowledge of such builders of *local* micro-climate is shown by the care with which they study the conditions for best orientation, although we have seen examples where this is determined by cosmological rather than climatic considerations. We have descriptions of how they study the site under all sorts of weather conditions and at all times of day, how they consider local wind patterns, misty or foggy locations, shady and sunny spots and their relation to the seasons, the movement of hot and cold air—and build their houses accordingly. In the description by Karen Blixen already discussed, the Africans placed their houses in relation to wind, sun, and shade as well as topography. In this case, each house was identical in form and type, whereas among European peasants, for example, although each house is basically like all the others in the area, there are individual variations to the model.

These builders work in an economy of scarcity, their resources of materials, energy, and technology are very limited, and the margin for error and waste correspondingly small, but the results show a high level of performance even when judged in the light of modern technology.[5] This also applies to early settlers in new countries who work under similar conditions. While immigrants often bring forms with them to which they cling with great tenacity in spite of unsuitability for the climate, adaptations to the new climate are finally made. One example would be the general increase in the eaves of roofs and the development of verandahs. This occurs in Quebec, where the small eaves gradually expanded and became verandahs and snow galleries, and the siting changed.[6] In Louisiana similar verandahs developed and windows increased, while in Australia the change was very similar (Fig. 4.1). The verandah provides sitting and sleeping space intermediate between outdoors and indoors (even when it rains), shades the walls and windows, and provides the possibility of continuing the ventilation of the house during violent rains.

[5] See James Marston Fitch and David P. Branch, "Primitive Architecture and Climate," *Scientific American,* CCVII, No. 6 (December 1960), 134-144; Victor Olgyay, *Design with Climate* (Princeton: Princeton University Press, 1963), the early chapters.

[6] See J. E. Aronin, *Climate and Architecture* (New York: Reinhold Publishing Corporation, 1953), p. 7.

The houses of early settlers of Australia, the United States, or Mexico are successful solutions, closer to the *attitudes* of primitive builders than to those of today, and the buildings are more successful, in terms of climate, than newer buildings in the same areas. We need only compare the snug, well-oriented houses of early New England, with their under-cover links to barn and store, the cool, breezy plantations of the South and the similar Australian forms, and the thick-walled patio-centered houses and haciendas of Mexico and the Southwestern United States with the corresponding houses in those areas today.

All these primitive and vernacular solutions show a great variety of designs related to conditions which surround a group of people living in an area, as well as the group's cultural and symbolic interpretations of these conditions and their definition of comfort. These houses are *not* individual solutions, but group solutions representative of a culture and its response to the characteristics of a region—its general climate and micro-climate, typical materials, and topography. The interaction of all these factors helps explain the similarity of solutions separated by thousands of years and miles, and the differences between solutions in apparently similar conditions and areas.

Nonmaterial Solutions

In addition to climatic solutions which are best analyzed in terms of orientation, structure, plan form, and materials, there are other approaches. One of these, while still involving the use of materials, can be viewed in terms of changing the dwelling at different times of the year on climatic grounds, as opposed to changes of a nonclimatic, or anticlimatic, character. In many cases the decision to use these alternative methods of coping with the problem may be socially motivated, although among, for example, the Eskimo, the change of dwelling type is affected by availability of materials during the different seasons as well as by the change in the climate.

Among the Paiute Indians, winter dwellings were conical structures with a central fire-pit and smoke hole, constructed of Juniper wood and bark covering or willow poles covered with dried brush or matting of reeds or grasses. These winter settlements also had a sweat house, which was also the men's meeting house and youths' dormitory and the most substantial dwelling in the settlement. During the warm season these settlements were usually deserted for unwalled square shades with flat roofs supported on four poles, or, more commonly, for circular or semi-circular windscreens of stakes and matting or brush against which sand might be piled up on the outside. Within the curve there would be a fireplace and sleeping places along the wall.

The herders of Siberia and Central Asia display a whole range of solutions of this type. Some use conical tents, similar to the tepees of North America, all year, but change from fur covering in the winter, with snow piled halfway up the tent for greater warmth, to hides in the summer. (This corresponds to the Mongol Yurt, where the number of layers of felt covering is changed depending on the season.) In other cases the variation between summer and winter dwelling is greater, with tents used during the summer and pit dwellings a few feet deep, covered with timber and sod, used during the winter.[7]

The whole pattern of settlement among the *Kazakhs* of Central Asia is modified by climate.[8] In the summer, pastures do not last long, mobility is necessary, and settlements of tents are dispersed on the hills. In the winter, protection from the severe cold and wind is gained by concentrating the settlements. Since this protection is even more critical for stock than for man, the settlements are placed in deep river valleys with a fringe of protecting woodlands. The tents remain strung out along the valleys even though the pastures may change.

Another Central Asian solution is to replace the summer tents with huts of stone, wood, or turf, depending on the area. These are rectangular and semidugout, with walls three feet thick, thick roofs, and animal membrane windows. A fire pit is placed near the front and late born animals settle around it; cooking and sleeping take place in the rear. Flanking the main dwelling are other huts for dependents, weak animals, and stores. Around the whole group stands a high wall of turf or reeds; a light roof of reeds on the inner side protects the remaining livestock. The basic form of these settlements seems to be determined more by the needs of livestock than of man.

Method of Study

There are several methods of approaching the study of the influence of climate on house form. One could look at the various climatic types—hot arid, hot humid, continental, temperate, arctic—and discuss the solutions typical of each in terms of requirements, forms, and materials. Alternatively, the positions of various house types along the climatic scale could be discussed, or, finally, one could consider how the several climatic variables which in combination result in the various climatic types are handled.

Climate, as it affects human comfort, is the result of air temperature, humidity, radiation—including light—air movement, and precipitation. To achieve comfort, these factors need to be handled in such a way as to establish some form of balance between the environmental stimuli so that the body is neither losing nor gaining too much heat, nor is subject to excessive stresses from other variables, although, as has been suggested, some stresses may be desirable. In climatic terms, therefore, a building needs to respond to heat, cold, ground and sky radiation, wind, and other

---

[7] Pit dwellings are, of course, found in many places and periods—among North American Indians, in Neolithic Japan, and in the Southwest of the United States; the *kiva* of the Pueblos is a formalized version of it, as was the roundhouse of the Southwest Pomo of California.

[8] As a comment on climatic determinism, it is interesting to compare this to the Mongols in the same area, who only change the covering on their Yurts. According to Spencer and Johnson, *Atlas for Anthropology* (Dubuque, Iowa: W. C. Brown Co., 1960), p. 23, both these peoples are in the Central Asian steppe area—the Mongols South of Lake Baikal, the Kazakhs between the Caspian, Aral, and Lake Balkash. Both areas have the same soil and climatic conditions, at least in gross terms.

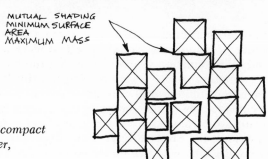

MUTUAL SHADING
MINIMUM SURFACE
AREA
MAXIMUM MASS

FIG. 4.2. Diagram showing compact
plan elements crowded together,
typical of hot, arid climates.

stresses, and the various parts of the building may be considered environmental control devices.

It is my intention to examine solutions to the various environmental forces in different areas, rather than use the more traditional method of describing "the classical mechanisms of thermal control" [9] for the principal climatic zones.

Climatic Variables and Responses to Them

The following variables will be considered:

temperature	heat—dry and humid; cold.
humidity	low, high.
wind	desirable or undesirable, and hence whether it should be encouraged or discouraged.
rain	comes mostly under construction, but involves climate by the need to keep out rain while retaining ventilation, especially in hot, humid areas.
radiation and light	desirable or undesirable, and hence whether it should be encouraged or discouraged.

While these could be arranged along the climatic scale according to severity, they will be examined for the responses they generate in terms of *form, materials, and devices.*

TEMPERATURE—DRY HEAT. Hot, dry areas are characterized by high daytime temperatures and uncomfortably low nighttime temperatures, a fluctuation best met by delaying the entry of heat as long as possible so that it will reach the interior late, when it is needed. This is achieved by use of high heat capacity materials, such as adobe or pisé, mud, stone, and various combinations of these which provide a "heat sink," absorbing heat during the day and reradiating it during the night; by as *compact a geometry* as possible, which provides maximum volume with minimum surface area exposed to the outside heat; by mutual crowding, which provides shading, and reduces the areas exposed to the sun while increasing the mass of the whole building group, thus increasing the time lag (Fig. 4.2). Heat buildup is avoided by separating cooking, often done outside the house; by reducing the number and size of windows and

[9] Fitch and Branch, "Primitive Architecture and Climate," p. 136.

placing them high up to reduce ground radiation; by painting the house white or some other light color to reflect a maximum of radiant heat; and by minimizing ventilation during the hot time of the day.[10]

Another device for increasing the dwelling's heat capacity is to use the almost infinite heat capacity of the earth. Dwellings can be built into a cliff face, as in the southwestern United States, southern Tunisia, the Loire Valley and southwest France. They can also be built underground, as among the Siwa of Egypt; the 10,000,000 people of Shansi and other areas of China who live underground; Israel, where we find whole underground villages 5,000 years old; the opal miners' houses in Australia; the "underground gardens" in Fresno, California; and the Matmata houses in the Sahara. In the latter every room is under a layer of earth at least 30 feet thick, the heat capacity is, in effect, infinite, and the house is cooler than anything which could be built on the surface (Fig. 4.3).

When the evenings are cool, people in hot, dry areas sleep on the roof or in the courtyard; when it is cold, they sleep inside. It is of interest that the Australian Building Research Station recommendation for hot arid areas is a great increase in the heat capacity of daytime living areas (that of most modern houses being too low), and a low heat capacity nighttime area. This corresponds to the traditional solution, of which the Punjab furnishes a typical example. The houses there, with thick mud walls and few openings, are constructed in an effort to keep out the sun; the result is that the interiors remain cool and dark all day. The roof or walled courtyard is used during the evening and warm nights, and the interior during cold ones. Outdoor sleeping—whether on the roof, in the court, or on the shaded verandahs of bungalows used by the wealthier people—is common. Many of the houses have two kitchens, one indoors for winter use and one outdoors for summer use. Since people work most of the day in the fields, summer living takes place largely outdoors, and the house becomes a storage space rather than a dwelling. However, if it were to be used during the day it would be very comfortable.

The court is also useful in coping with the dry heat itself, and has climatic implications as well as the social and psychological ones already discussed. It gives protection from sandstorms. When it is provided with greenery and water, and is shaded, it acts as a cooling well and actually modifies the micro-climate by lowering ground temperatures and radiation and by evaporation. The use of greenery and water in a court also has soothing and cooling psychological effects in a hot arid area, and helps provide an outdoor living area. When a shady court is used in conjunction with a sunny court, in which the heated air will rise, cool air may flow from the shady court into the sunny one through the rooms.

If the court is made high, as in the tall buildings of the Hadhramaut,

---

[10] This use of "programmed ventilation"—opening the house when the outside is cool and keeping it tightly closed when it is hot—only works if the time lag is high. When this cannot be achieved, it is often preferable to go to the other extreme and allow maximum ventilation, even though the air is very hot. This is what is done in the Arab tent, which cannot use heat capacity. A research project on low cost housing in a hot, dry area in which I was involved came to the same conclusion. See H. Sanoff, T. Porter, and A. Rapoport, *Low Income Housing Demonstration* (Dept. of Architecture, University of California, Berkeley, November 1965).

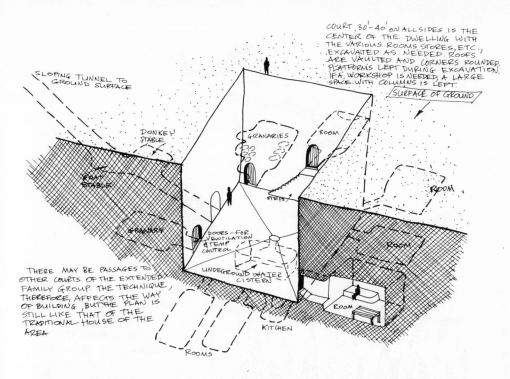

Labels in figure:

SLOPING TUNNEL TO GROUND SURFACE

COURT, 30'-40' ON ALL SIDES IS THE CENTER OF THE DWELLING WITH THE VARIOUS ROOMS, STORES, ETC., EXCAVATED AS NEEDED. ROOFS ARE VAULTED AND CORNERS ROUNDED. PLATFORMS LEFT DURING EXCAVATION. IF A WORKSHOP IS NEEDED, A LARGE SPACE WITH COLUMNS IS LEFT.

SURFACE OF GROUND

DONKEY STABLE

GRANARIES

ROOM

GOAT STABLE

ROOM

GRANARY

STEPS

DOORS - FOR VENTILATION & TEMP CONTROL

ROOM

THERE MAY BE PASSAGES TO OTHER COURTS OF THE EXTENDED FAMILY GROUP. THE TECHNIQUE, THEREFORE, AFFECTS THE WAY OF BUILDING, BUT THE PLAN IS STILL LIKE THAT OF THE TRADITIONAL HOUSE OF THE AREA

UNDEGROUND WATER CISTERN

ROOM

KITCHEN

ROOMS

FIG. 4.3. *Cutaway view of Matmata dwelling, Sahara. (Adapted from a number of sources, primarily Haan in* Architects' Yearbook 11 *and* New Frontiers in Architecture.*)*

Southern Arabia, and cross ventilation encouraged at the top by slots in a projecting "chimney," suction can be produced and some cross ventilation induced. This method has many local variants throughout that part of Arabia.

When we consider the materials used, it could be asked whether these heavy walls are created by deliberate intent, or are simply the result of the materials found, such as stone and mud, which demand heavy walls structurally. In many areas, however, other materials, such as palm logs, are found, and open shady shelters could be built without the heavy mud roof. For example, the Ashanti hut in Africa provides clear evidence of deliberate use of heavy walls and roofs for climatic reasons. These huts employ a wooden skeleton frame carrying a roof of twigs, on top of which is a roof of beaten mud the purpose of which is clearly climatic control, since it is structurally unreasonable. Moreover, the walls, which in terms of structure are curtain walls and do no bearing, are of extremely heavy, thick mud construction (Fig. 4.4). This solution seems inescapably to be climatically motivated, although such a social aspect as Arab influence might be possible. The climatic rationale is even more likely when it is noted that Ashanti huts in more extreme areas have thicker walls in order to increase heat capacity, and are even built into cliff

FIG. 4.4.
Cutaway view
of Ashanti hut.

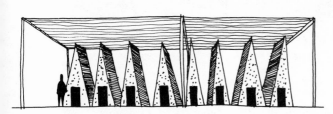

FIG. 4.5. Yokut settle-
ment showing continuous
brushwood shade.
(Adapted from Morgan,
Houses and House Life
of the American
Aborigines, p. 112.)

faces; in more moderate areas, where there is less temperature variation, the mass of these walls is reduced by combining the mud with ever greater amounts of vegetable fibers.

A similar question could be raised with regard to the compact plan, or use of buildings crowded together: to what extent is this done to reduce the surface area exposed to the sun and increase shading, and to what extent to preserve valuable land, to provide for defense needs, and so on? These purposes undoubtedly play a role, as do social and family requirements, but instances of the deliberate use of shading can be found; for example, the Yokuts of Southern California shaded the whole settlement (Fig. 4.5). Another instance is the widespread use of double roofs, found among the Massa of the Cameroons, on the Bauchi plateau of Nigeria, and in India (Fig. 4.6), as well as the double walls of New Caledonia.

FIG. 4.6. Double roof in Orissa, India.

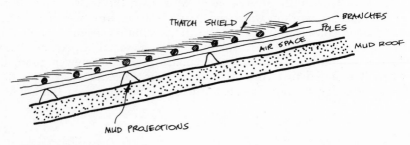

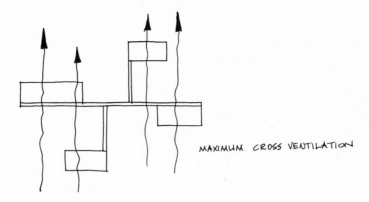

FIG. 4.7. *Diagram showing the long, narrow geometry and wide spacing typical of a hot, humid climate.*

The double roof has four consequences:

1. Thatch sheds water and protects the mud in the rainy season (see Chapter 5).
2. The thatch shades the mud roof from the direct sun, reducing heat build-up and hence the heating up of the house.
3. The airspace provides additional insulation during the hot days, while the heat capacity of the mud keeps down the day temperatures.
4. The mud conserves the heat for cold nights, and the thatch helps it conserve that heat for a longer portion of the night by reducing heat loss to the cold sky.

Thatch alone would be sufficient structurally, and even for rain protection, but the mud is clearly used for its thermal properties, and the combination is very effective. There is also a climatic component in the use of verandahs in various areas, as well as in the use of shutters, but the choice among these different solutions, as has already been suggested, is culturally determined.

TEMPERATURE—HUMID HEAT. Humid heat areas are characterized by heavy rainfall, high humidity, relatively moderate temperatures with little daily or seasonal variation, and intense radiation. The required responses are maximum shade and minimum heat capacity. Heat storage has no advantage when there is little temperature variation, and heavy construction will hinder maximum ventilation, which is the primary requirement for helping the body lose heat. The requirements, almost the exact opposite of those for dry heat, call for open, low heat capacity buildings with maximum cross ventilation, and hence long narrow geometry and widely separated forms, with walls at a minimum (Fig. 4.7).

The need for openness creates problems of privacy, particularly acoustic privacy. Cultures where such openness is essential often tolerate very high noise levels and accept less acoustic privacy, as in Singapore, or develop social controls, as did the Yagua. (This need also creates problems with regard to light, which I will discuss later.) The need for

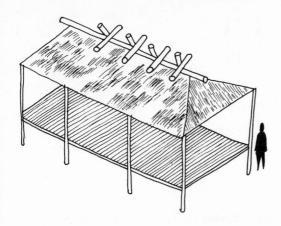

FIG. 4.8. Seminole house, Florida (approximately 9 ft x 16 ft in plan).

openness extends to the floor, and in Malaya or among the Yagua, for instance, the use of split bamboo floors, combined with raised houses, allows air to flow from below. Hammocks, often used for sleeping, also help the flow of air from below, and, as one swings, air flow past the body is encouraged with little effort. The hammock, unlike a mattress, which can quickly become unbearable, has negligible heat capacity.

The traditional solutions are fully in accord with recent climatological studies. The roof becomes the dominant element in these houses and is, in effect, a huge, waterproof parasol, sloping steeply to shed torrential rains, opaque to solar radiation, and of minimum mass to avoid heat build-up and subsequent reradiation. It also avoids condensation problems by being able to "breathe." Deep overhangs are protection against both sun and rain, and also allow ventilation during rain. The floor is often raised, not only for religious reasons but also for better exposure to breezes, for flood protection, and as a defense against the large insect and animal population. A typical example is the Seminole house of Florida, with its floor three feet above the ground, palmetto thatch roof, and open sides with moveable bark sheets (Fig. 4.8). Houses of this type are much more comfortable than the wooden, brick, or stone houses with tin roofs which are replacing them in the same areas.

I have already referred to the Yagua dwelling; [11] the Melanesian dwelling displays the same elements. It has either no walls, with a drop-down screen of woven coconut palm leaf, or open walls of vertically spaced mid-ribs of similar leaves. The most extreme example of this type of solution is the minimum house in Colombia, which is just a grass roof on a framework which also supports the hammock, various storage baskets, sacks, and so on (Fig. 4.9).

In contrast, there are areas where the expected solution is not found. The Maya have windowless stone houses in a hot, humid climate, while the Japanese house does not use its design as effectively as one would expect. However, in many diverse areas the principles described as

[11] Amos Rapoport, "Yagua, or the Amazon Dwelling," *Landscape,* XVI, No. 3 (Spring 1967), 27-30.

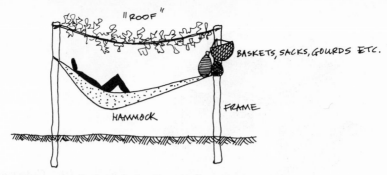

FIG. 4.9. *Minimum shelter, Colombia. (Adapted from* Housing, Building, and Planning, *No. 8, Nov., 1953, p. 91.)*

optimal for the conditions are in effect, although the specific forms may be different. In Haiti, for example, houses may have solid walls and large French doors for ventilation, or, alternatively, use walls of split bamboo, while dormers in the roof may overhang the house and trap each breeze, helping ventilation and expelling hot air.

In Moslem areas like Pakistan and in North India, where the need for at least visual privacy becomes socially important because of the attitudes toward women, but where ventilation is essential to cope with humid heat, the development of open-work screens ("Jali") has taken place. These provide shade and privacy for women while allowing effective cross ventilation. In these same areas, where the humid heat is only seasonal, high ceilings of 15 to 20 feet in urban houses allow cool air in at night during the hot, dry season and, in effect, store it during the day. This has little effect during the hot, humid season as long as cross ventilation is allowed, but is a disadvantage during the cold winters, when such rooms become difficult to heat.[12]

TEMPERATURE—COLD. There are different degrees of cold, and variations of intensity and duration, but the principles for keeping warm are the same and relate closely to those for arid heat. The same principles apply, except that the source of heat is now *inside* rather than outside, and the attempt to stop heat flow is in the opposite direction. Attempts are made to heat the dwelling as well as possible, involving large stove elements often found at the center of the house, to use the heat of cooking, and that given off by people and, sometimes, animals. The loss of heat is avoided by use of a compact plan, minimum surface area exposed to the outside, heavy materials of good insulating capacity, and prevention of drafts and air leaks. Snow, a very good insulator, is often encouraged to build up in thick layers on roofs, and thus affects the form, size, and strength of roofs. The only other difference from hot, arid areas may be the desire to capture as much solar radiation as possible, and therefore dark colors are used. However, this desire is often outweighed

[12] "Islamabad," *Architectural Review,* CXLI, No. 841 (March 1967), 212.

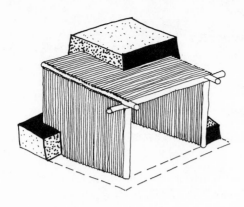

FIG. 4.10. Cutaway view of Siberian timber and sod house.

by the need to shelter from the wind and reduce the surface area exposed to the cold, so compact grouping and subterranean or semisubterranean dwellings are frequently encountered.

In considering attempts to solve these problems, it is difficult to avoid discussing the Igloo and other Eskimo solutions. The need to cope with intense, steady cold and high winds has led to the Igloo, built of dry snow, but used only by the Central Eskimo. The Greenland and Alaskan Eskimo build their winter homes of stone and sod, and use the Igloo only as an overnight shelter while hunting. The attempt in all these cases is to offer least resistance to wind, and provide a maximum volume with a minimum surface area. The hemisphere of the Igloo does that perfectly, as well as being most efficiently heated by a seal-oil lamp, a point source of radiant heat which the hemisphere helps focus at the center.

The refinements of the Igloo could be discussed at great length, but since it has been widely described and analyzed, only the floor raised above the tunnel entrance will be mentioned. This excludes drafts, and, since warm air rises and cold air sinks, the people inside are kept in a warmer zone. During the summer, semiunderground dwellings with a plan similar to that of the Igloo are used. Walls are of stone or sod five feet six inches high, the entry is narrow and underground, and the floor is, once again, at a higher level than the entry. Rafters of whale ribs or driftwood are covered by a double layer of sealskin with moss between, which constitutes an effective sandwich panel.

Awareness of the need for solutions required for cold can be seen in a way analogous to the Ashanti example discussed before. The Yakut of Siberia, for example, as well as some Eskimo, use timber frame construction, covered with wood and then a heavy layer of sod (Fig. 4.10). This stops the wind better and is warmer than a log cabin, which has many cracks difficult to caulk and windproof, but it is structurally unreasonable and is a response to climatic needs.

The Irish stone house, low and hugging the ground, is also a good response to a cold and windswept area, and similar variations on the theme are found elsewhere. Peasants in Switzerland keep their cattle in the house, which provides additional heat as well as making it easier to get to them in cold, snowy weather without going outside, although this can also be solved by covered links—as on the farms of New England. Development of arcaded streets in northern towns of Japan shows the importance of winter circulation in affecting plan form; this, and the underground links between Eskimo Igloos, are similar to equivalent solutions in hot dry areas, as, for example, the underground tunnel connections of the Matmata and the shaded streets of Arab towns.

During the cold, snowy winters the air can be rather humid, which condition, combined with the very low temperatures, may make the drying of clothing and other articles a major problem. This is also a problem in the humid tropics, but can be handled by using the outdoors and totally open houses. In cold areas this becomes impossible since it is too cold to open the whole house, the outside cannot be used, and, in many areas, privacy requirements would preclude the use of open houses. We therefore find drying rooms near the large stove, or drying galleries and open lofts as, for example, in the Savoie, France, where balconies 12 feet deep are used for the drying of clothes and vegetables.

HUMIDITY. High and low humidity have been considered with the corresponding types of heat because temperature and humidity operate together as regards comfort. Where humidity is high, little can be done to reduce it by nonmechanical means, and ventilation is used to help the body lose heat. Where humidity is low, water and vegetation can be used to increase it, as well as humidifying devices which often involve the trickling of water over either grass matting in the windows, or porous pottery, as found in traditional houses in India and Egypt.

WIND. Wind is also related to temperature and, in fact, windspeed, humidity, and temperature all enter into the concept of *effective temperature* which is used to measure comfort. The need for comfort leads either to encouraging or discouraging wind. When it is cold, or very dry, wind generally becomes undesirable; when it is hot and humid, wind is essential.

The most primitive device for controlling wind is the windbreak, found in a number of areas—among the aborigines of Australia, who use both branch and kangaroo skin windbreaks, the Semang in Malaya (Fig. 4.11), and American Indians. The Arab tent uses the backstrip, which is

FIG. 4.11. Semang windbreak shelter.

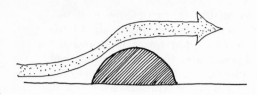
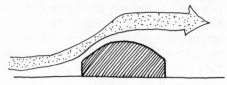

IGLOO   YURT

FIG. 4.12.   *Wind and the forms of Igloo and Yurt.*

moved around as needed to block or encourage wind, and in Melanesia, Samoa, and among the Khoisan of South Africa, wall panels are either lowered, raised, or moved around to different positions to block wind or to let it in. Since it is generally easier to capture wind than to avoid it, I will consider the latter aspect in more detail. A comparison, however, of the Japanese house with the adobe of New Mexico, or the Yagua house with the Arab house, enables us to grasp immediately the basic differences in form entailed by encouraging or discouraging wind.

As we would expect, areas with severe problems show the most forceful solutions. Both the Eskimos and the Mongols live in areas of extreme winds, particularly during the winter, and both the Igloo and the Yurt represent extremely successful solutions approximating (especially the Igloo) a hemisphere, the advantages of which I have already discussed (Fig. 4.12). We have also seen the measures taken by the herders of Central Asia both in terms of shelter and siting. The Eskimo also take very elaborate precautions with regard to siting, selecting the most sheltered spots, with the Igloos facing the beach (the sea being the main source of food) in the lee of raised cliffs (Fig. 4.13).

Entry to the Igloo is through a tunnel which is curved to keep out wind. One main entrance is used for a group of dwellings linked by interior passages, thus enabling more effective buffering against the wind. The tunnel is provided with transitional spaces where the air is tempered, and the raised floor also helps avoid the wind. The entry may be parallel to the wind direction, which helps avoid the direct wind, or it may be on

FIG. 4.13.   *Location of Eskimo village.*

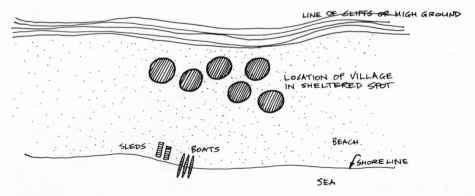

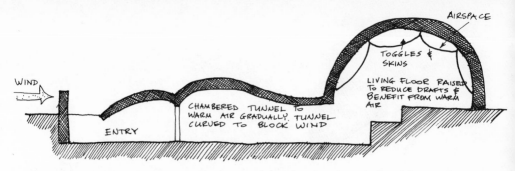

FIG. 4.14.   *Diagrammatic section through Igloo (much detail left out).*

FIG. 4.15.   *Tepee,*
showing wind control flaps.

the windward side, protected by a low snow block wall, since on the lee snowdrifts become a problem (Fig. 4.14).

Wind in the Plains Indians' tepee could be controlled by means of two projecting tongues, or ears, supported by two large poles inserted into pockets. These could be set wide apart, by adjusting the poles, so as to admit air and breezes in fine weather, or drawn together to exclude wind and rain, or retain heat during the night (Fig. 4.15).

In Normandy, where winds are also a problem, farmhouses have thatched roofs which in form resemble the hull of a ship turned upside down, with the bow facing the wind, west, and the stern open to the calm, sheltered east (Fig. 4.16).

FIG. 4.16.   *Farm in Normandy.*
(Adapted from Grillo,
What Is Design? *p. 106*
and author's observations.)

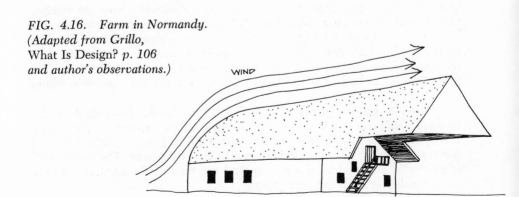

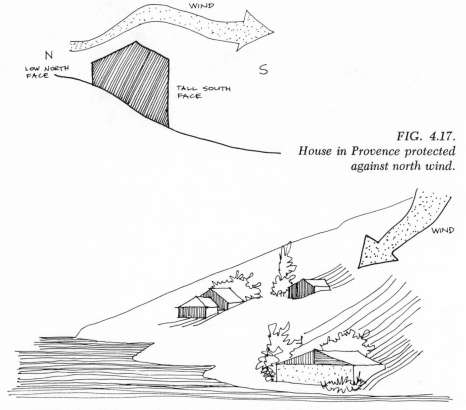

FIG. 4.17.
House in Provence protected
against north wind.

FIG. 4.18. Houses located for maximum protection
against cold winds in Switzerland. (Adapted from Weiss,
Häuser und Landschaften der Schweiz, p. 188.)

In many other areas houses are sited to avoid or maximize the wind. We can see this in Canada, in Mexico, where siting has been codified by the Law of the Indies as well as by tradition, in Ireland, and in Tristan da Cunha, where the stone houses are half sunk into the ground to escape gales. Provence, generally a warm area, has a cold wind from the north—the Mistral. Houses are placed in hollows so that the north wall is one story high and either blank or with very few openings, while the wall facing south is two storys high and has many windows protected by shutters, since there are few shade trees in the area (Fig. 4.17). Open porches are also used in lieu of shade trees. Similar siting is used in Switzerland (Fig. 4.18).

Barns in Oregon display a similar approach—the long slant of the roof faces into the wind, with eaves very low off the ground. In the winter this space is filled with bales of hay or alfalfa to form a continuation of the snow blanket which is encouraged to cover the roof. The south wall is painted a dark red to absorb sun, and the heat of the animals and the snow insulation keep the barn warm.

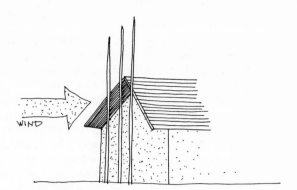

FIG. 4.19. Windpoles in Switzerland, used to protect the house against the force of the wind. (Adapted from Weiss, Häuser und Landschaften der Schweiz, pp. 96-97.)

Special windpoles, which stood in front of the house and broke the force of the wind,[13] were once very common in Switzerland (Fig. 4.19). In other areas this effect is achieved by planting windbreaks in front of and around houses. These groups of trees become very dominant in the landscape, and also act as housemarkers in the flat plain.

RAIN. The main effects of rain are on the construction of houses, which will be discussed in Chapter 5. In arid areas, catching rain and protecting it from evaporation may be important, as in some Caribbean islands, where cisterns under the houses are used. In the Trulli of Italy these cisterns are accessible directly from the house and may have a cooling effect on the house and help to humidify it.

In hot, humid areas, wide eaves or verandahs allowing windows to be left open for ventilation while it rains, become the principal climatic form-modifying element. Some tribes in Natal, South Africa, actually use rain to help control the weather response of the house. They build houses of a light frame which is sheathed in woven mats. The weave contracts in dry weather, permitting the movement of air through the interstices, but the fibers expand in wet weather, converting them into nearly waterproof and windproof membranes.

RADIATION AND LIGHT. Radiation and light are generally undesirable in hot areas, and various devices are used to avoid them. In cold areas, particularly in the winter, light and radiation are desirable, and although large openings may create problems of cold and heat loss, they are often used, as, for example, in Holland and Norway. The Eskimo use a window of ice or skin directly facing whatever winter sun there is, while during the long summer day they use dark tents to exclude the light.

In hot, dry areas, as we have seen, direct radiation of the sun is avoided in various ways. This is another example of choice, since once the need for excluding excess light has been decided upon—and the definition of "excess" is variable—there are many different solutions possible, and each culture handles the problem in its own way. The same

[13] Richard Weiss, *Häuser und Landschaften der Schweiz* (Erlenbach-Zurich: Eugen Rentsch Verlag, 1959), pp. 96-97.

goal can be achieved by having few and small openings, as in North Africa; by having sizeable windows with dark shutters, as in Spain and Italy; by the wide overhangs, lack of walls, and dark materials of the Yagua dwelling; or by the wide verandahs of Louisiana or Australia (now replaced by picture windows). Verandahs and overhangs can be designed to allow the low winter sun to enter while excluding the higher summer sun, as has been traditional in Japan, Aden, Zanzibar, and Ancient Greece.

Another important component in hot, dry areas is ground radiation, which can be a major source of glare and heat where there is no vegetative ground cover. Openings tend to be placed high to avoid this, or shaded arcades used around the house, and attempts are made to use vegetation and water around the house, although this is often difficult. In some areas deciduous trees are planted; as they lose their leaves in winter they admit the sun, which is excluded by the foliage in the summer. They also cool the immediate setting of the house through transpiration, evaporation, shading, and reflections. Externally in such areas we find the use of geometric forms which stand out in the sun without glaring reflections. Attempts are sometimes made to shade entire settlements, as the Southern Californian example already discussed, and whole streets and markets are shaded in Spain, Japan, Arab countries, and North Africa. Shadows generally attract people in these areas, and settlements were traditionally designed with this in mind.

The problem of glare in the humid tropics can be worse than the full sun of the desert. The milky sky creates an almost unbearable glare, which is one reason for having walls permeable to the wind in these areas, rather than not having any walls at all; privacy may be another reason.

FIG. 4.20. Malay house.

Walls of vertically spaced or woven bamboo, as in Malaya, allow light quality good enough for delicate weaving while completely eliminating glare in a way that no window could. This is also the principle behind the pierced screens of India, Pakistan, and elsewhere, to which I have already referred. In addition to allowing ventilation while giving privacy to women who can see out without being seen, the screens also reduce glare by reducing the apparent brightness of sky and ground. The lattices of Sewun in the Hadhramaut and other Arab countries, and the light-weight shaded verandahs, with lattices, of Zanzibar, have the same function, while the latter also overhang and shade the sidewalks. In some Malayan houses low eaves and wide verandahs offer protection from sky glare as well as from sun and rain, while allowing cross ventilation, and white ceilings give good distribution to the light which is admitted (Fig. 4.20).

CHAPTER **5** *construction, materials,*
and technology as modifying factors

The decision as to what form the house shall take is made on socio-cultural grounds—way of life, shared group values, and "ideal" environment sought. But once it has been decided whether the dwelling is to be individual or communal, permanent or portable, the whole setting for life or part of the larger realm of the settlement; once adaptation to site has been made, and the form has responded to climatic forces, there still remain certain universal problems—those relating to construction.

To create any type of place, space must be enclosed. The availability and choice of materials and construction techniques in an architectural situation will greatly influence and modify the form of the building. In the same way that the house responds to the physical stresses of climate—heat, cold, humidity, radiation, and light—it must also respond structurally to the mechanical stresses—gravity, wind, rain, and snow. The reason why construction (which, of course, involves technology) and materials are best regarded as modifying factors, in spite of their fundamental nature, is that they do not determine form. They merely make possible forms which have been selected on other grounds, they make certain forms *impossible*, and, in acting as a tool, they modify forms.

One of the basic problems of architecture, and the principal problem of construction, is *the spanning of space*—the collection of gravitational forces and their transmission to the ground, usually requiring materials having reasonable tensile strength and a reasonable weight-strength ratio.[1] Under primitive conditions, these are limited to organic materials either animal in origin (bone, skin, and felts) or vegetable (timber or plaited,

[1] The problem of spanning space is avoided by people who use the windbreak; the use of natural caves also avoids it. Even where caves are manmade—as in Spain, the Loire Valley, Cappadocia, China, and North Africa—the problem is different, since the material is almost by definition suitable for the purpose.

woven, or twisted vegetable fibers in such forms as matting, textiles, and rope). The only addition in the preindustrial vernacular is an occasional small quantity of metal. Where no such materials are available, or are difficult to obtain, special forms of construction—e.g., beehive vaults and domes, true vaults and domes—have been developed. In some cases, as that of the pueblos, the need for materials with tensile strength has meant bringing timber great distances. Because of its scarcity the beams have been used full-length, so that portions project; these beams are removed and reused many times.

The primitive and peasant milieu is characterized by an economy of scarcity of materials which can be severe. The Eskimo has only snow and ice, fur and bone, and some driftwood; the Sudanese have mud, reeds, and some palm logs; the Siberian herdsman has only felted hair, hides, and small amounts of wood, while the Uru of Peru (Lake Titicaca) and the marsh dwellers of Iraq have only reeds. While this scarcity does not determine form, it does make some solutions *impossible* and reduces the choice to an extent, depending on the severity of the limitations. Together with the limitations of technology, it has considerable effects on form, since the possible variety is reduced. This exemplifies the concept of the *scale of criticality*, paralleling those relating to climate and wealth.

The more extreme the constraints, the less the choice, but some choice is always available. Constraints make it necessary to provide spaces desired for various human activities by the most direct means. Limited materials and techniques, used to their ultimate, must be used to define place. Typically, under such conditions, builders will work up to the technological limits at their disposal, while we, with almost unlimited means, tend to work well below ours.[2] Primitive builders are able to conserve their materials because they have detailed and precise knowledge of the behavior and characteristics of materials, not just in terms of climatic response and construction, but also in regard to weathering—how the materials and building fabric will stand up to the ravages of time and weather. This understanding tends to lead to clear, straightforward solutions to the problems posed by gravity and weathering.

This chapter deals with these universal problems of the enclosing of space; weathering, wind forces, and portability; the ways in which different people have solved them; and the form consequences these solutions may have. Socio-cultural, climatic, and visual aspects of the problem will not be discussed here. The stress will be on the ingenuity of solutions, their success in achieving maximum effect with minimum means, thoughtful and direct designs, sophistication of efforts, and the effect of all this on the forms of buildings.

Even here some solutions will be structurally irrational, which is fully analogous with the anticlimatic examples, although their number seems fewer, possibly because the imperatives are more stringent. One example is the flat roof carried on cross beams, which is a common form found over an immense area. Structurally, the roof should be as light as possible and the dead weight of the structure kept to a minimum. In hot areas,

[2] A. H. Brodrick, "Grass Roots," *Architectural Review*, CXV, No. 686 (February 1954), 101-111.

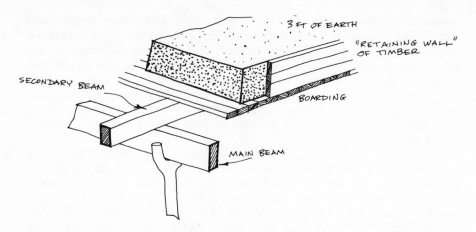

FIG. 5.1.   Roof of Iranian house (near Shiraz).

however, heavy earth roofs which increase the time lag of heating, but
are structurally unreasonable, are used. We have already noted the example of the Ashanti hut, and the same kind of construction can be seen
in some Iranian houses, where slender wooden columns carry a roof
which supports three feet of earth covered with grass or tiles to protect
it from the rain (Fig. 5.1). Since the heavy mud walls are also not required structurally, climatic control is clearly the object, and structural
efficiency is low.

Since the number of solutions, at least in principle, is limited, it can
be said that every form of construction can be found in primitive and vernacular building, including many structural concepts considered new.
Not only are there the relatively simple mud and stone bearing walls of
ancient Jericho and Çatal Hüyük, and the log and thatch construction of
Biskupin (Poland), but also frame construction and curtain walls, of
which there are many examples dating from prehistory; continuously
poured structures, as in the pueblos; prefabrication, found in Africa and
Asia; tension structures, such as the Arab tent; and space frames, as in
the Yagua dwelling. All the elements of building—walls, roofs, doors,
windows, and so on—can be found in their most direct, early form. Indeed,
if we wish, the development of these elements into high-style architecture
can be traced; in Iran, some of the forms of Persepolis relate to vernacular
forms. In turn, high style can influence the vernacular, as in the village
Baroque of Austria and Switzerland.

Since the objective of construction is the enclosing of space, essential
in the making of usable places, the problem is basically one of spanning
space while limiting the mass of the building in plan and section. This
objective, in combination with the limitations discussed, means that the
way in which space is bridged affects form considerably, but does not
determine it. For example, vaults, which solve some of these problems,
were known in Ancient Egypt, but were used only where they could
not be seen, since they were at odds with the popular image of buildings;

at the same time, the large mass of supporting columns in temples was deliberately exaggerated by staggering.[3] In houses this could not be done, since required activity spaces had more utilitarian criticality than temples.

I will give a few examples out of the many possible for each of the principal types of construction discussed, and make some comments about related matters. The following problems and their various solutions will be considered:

the process of construction   Differentiation of trades, cooperation, and so on.
materials—basis for choice
portability
prefabrication
lateral forces
weathering
gravity   The major problem and various solutions to it—pure tensile, frame, compression, vertical load–carrying elements.

The Process of Construction

I have already referred to the progressive differentiation of trades as primitive building develops into preindustrial vernacular. There are even some instances of specialization among primitive people, with such dwellings as chiefs' houses in the South Seas built by tradesmen while the majority of houses are built by their inhabitants. Peasants in general are not merely agriculturalists, since they have to dress themselves, make containers and tools, and build houses. Specialist builders are more typical among peasants than among primitive people, although both tradesmen and the people become involved in the building task side by side, and the tradesmen are only part-time experts.

The custom of cooperative building not only helps overcome complex building tasks, but also has social implications, as we have seen in the Cebuan dwelling in the Philippines. If social aspects lead to cooperative construction, certain complex or difficult techniques and forms become possible. The Fon of Dahomey, for example, have a cooperative work group, the Dopkwe, to which all males of the village belong. This group aids the three tasks best performed by group labor—making a farm, building a wall, and roofing a house—and while the host normally provides food for the group, those who are sick, old, or poor need not provide a feast; [4] their society assures them of a minimum for survival. Such building tasks as prefabrication of a roof, which is then transported to the house and hoisted in place, obviously need cooperative effort. This practice is fairly common in Africa, Indochina, Melanesia, among the American Indians, in the Nicobar islands (Bay of Bengal), and in the United States—consider the New England hoisting party and the Midwestern barn raising.

Among the Kabyles, both tradesmen and the people are involved in a cooperative effort which has received special attention.[5] The Kabyles

[3] Siegfried Giedion, *The Eternal Present*, Vol. 2 (New York: Pantheon Books, Inc., 1964), pp. 389, 508-509, 514-515.
[4] Exhibition at Kroeber Hall, University of California, Berkeley, March 1967.
[5] R. Maunier, *La Construction Collective de la Maison en Kabylie* (Paris: Insitut d'ethnologie, 1926). The whole book deals with the topic.

live in stone houses with tile roofs whose construction is a complex task. While tradesmen are involved, the family and the communal group bear primary responsibility, and family, neighbors, and friends all help in an example of truly collective building. While this cooperation may be due to the need to build a complex house which could not be built otherwise, and could be an economic matter, the need for social cooperation may precede the use of complex forms and, indeed, make them possible. Construction of the house involves two distinct phases: preparation, when the site is selected, and materials gathered and brought to the site; and building, when the house is actually completed. The two social groups involved in the task are the domestic, related by blood (family), and the village group (the community). The extended family group, which expresses its unity by living together around a common court, is the primary work group. Men, women, and children all help, which expresses the family unity in economic and social terms. This is not enough to complete the job, however, and the communal group is called in as demanded by both building tasks and ritual. As in most primitive and peasant cultures, construction has important ritual and religious aspects; technical action is associated with mystical action. Both the building and ritual tasks are prolonged and complex, and it cannot be assumed that the technical takes precedence over the ritual. Material and spiritual actions are linked through rites of construction which take place at various points in the process—much as they do in Japan, the South Seas, China, and Scandinavia. This procedure forms part of the complex, multiple activity represented by house building, with collective work as its essence. Everyone participates in building, and specialized work, while it exists, is unusual.

Materials—Basis for Choice

It has been suggested that primitive and preindustrial vernacular builders always use materials most conveniently available, and that, since materials determine form, the nature of local materials determines form. These oversimple beliefs are not necessarily true; it has already been shown that the same materials may produce very different forms. However, the question of whether local materials are necessarily used has not yet been discussed. While in most cases such materials will, obviously, be utilized, this is far from being the case universally.

There are many instances where choice of materials is determined by the tendency to use permanent solid materials, such as stone, for cult buildings and tombs, while houses are built of more perishable materials.[6] This practice is found in Assam, pre-Columbian America, and in many areas of the South Seas, where chiefs' houses, canoe houses, and temples are built of stone while dwellings are built of wood.

However, the situation in the case of dwellings is far more complex than is commonly realized. Some primitive people actually grow materials

---

[6] Pierre Deffontaines, *Géographie et Religions*, 9th ed. (Paris: Librairie Gallimard, 1948), p. 36, states this as almost a universal rule, and applies it to many areas. Lord Raglan, *The Temple and the House* (New York: W. W. Norton & Company, 1964), p. 178, makes the same point, and gives a number of examples.

especially for building. In the South Seas, the sago palms grown near the villages are meant more for leaves to be used in building than for food. There are also many areas where it cannot be assumed that only local materials will be used. For example, houses in the west Valais area of France are of stone while those of the east Valais are of timber, although both materials are equally available in both areas. In Caux and around Caen, where timber is lacking and stone plentiful, wooden houses are found, while stone houses are found in richly wooded parts of Normandy. In Aydat and Puy-de-Dôme, where there is so much stone that field walls have to be built of it in order to clear the fields, houses were built of wood until the nineteenth century.[7]

It remains true that what is not available cannot be used, which is another example of *negative* impact—of things becoming impossible rather than inevitable. Because of the low criticality a choice exists, and use of materials is decided by fashion, tradition, religious proscription, or prestige value. The scale at which we examine the use of materials is of great importance. Vidal de la Blache, for example, shows a map of the use of materials in Europe which indicates that most of France, except for Normandy, uses stone, which would eliminate the variations just discussed.[8]

As an example of the effect on housing of changes in fashion, houses in one area of Monmouthshire, Wales, were built of wood until the end of the seventeenth century, and thereafter were built of stone, although timber was still available. The impact of tradition can be seen in Herefordshire, where wood was used until the end of the seventeenth century although stone was available, and in Devonshire, where houses were of "cob" (mud) until recently, even though both wood and stone were available. Conditions in Devonshire were like those on the Welsh border, where no mud houses are to be found.[9]

Religious proscriptions may also affect the use of materials. Brick and tile were prohibited for houses in some areas of India, whereas for temples wood was forbidden, except for the door.[10] Another basis of choice may be prestige value, already discussed in connection with the use of galvanized iron in Malaya, Peru, and elsewhere. Materials which involve a great deal of effort or labor may be prestigious, and hence favored by rulers and priests. Certain materials may be related to those used in a previous habitat prior to migration, and thus represent archaic survivals. We have already seen the tenacity with which migrants cling to old dwelling forms in new areas, and this also applies to materials. A good example of such practices is California, where the Spanish in the northern

---

[7] See Raglan, *The Temple and the House*, Chap. XIX, pp. 175 ff. He gives examples of areas which import wood or stone while the other is plentiful—the south Dauphiné, Haute Savoie, and so on.

[8] Vidal de la Blache, *Principes de la Géographie Humaine* (Paris: Armand Colin, 1922).

[9] Raglan, *The Temple and the House*, p. 176.

[10] *Ibid.*, pp. 178-179, where many examples are given. See also Deffontaines, *Géographie et Religions*, pp. 38 ff. and 83-86, where many examples are given of the impact of religion on the choice of materials unrelated to local availability, climate, and so forth.

counties use adobe, the Russians use logs, and the Americans build with frame construction; little stone is used by any of them in spite of its availability.

Portability

Problems created by the need for portability seem very constraining, yet there are a great number of solutions, ranging from tents of various sorts to large dwellings like those of the Northwest Indians and the overnight Igloo used by Eskimos when hunting. Portability is, of course, affected by the means of transport; the tepee got larger when the horse became available to help transport it. I will discuss two very different portable dwellings in order to show the variety of structural solutions possible.

The most elaborate of all the tents, which are themselves almost a symbol of portability, is the Mongol Yurt. Each Yurt is used by one family and is sparsely furnished. Cooking utensils are kept in a gaily painted wooden chest which doubles as a sideboard for ornaments. Since the materials available are felt and a small amount of wood, the structural

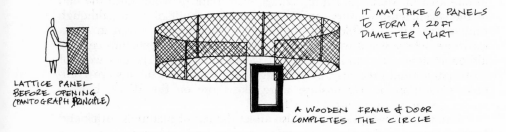

LATTICE PANEL BEFORE OPENING (PANTOGRAPH PRINCIPLE)

IT MAY TAKE 6 PANELS TO FORM A 20 FT DIAMETER YURT

A WOODEN FRAME & DOOR COMPLETES THE CIRCLE

FIG. 5.2.   *Erection of Yurt, stage 1.*

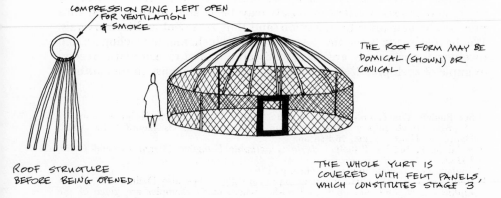

COMPRESSION RING LEFT OPEN FOR VENTILATION & SMOKE

THE ROOF FORM MAY BE DOMICAL (SHOWN) OR CONICAL

ROOF STRUCTURE BEFORE BEING OPENED

THE WHOLE YURT IS COVERED WITH FELT PANELS, WHICH CONSTITUTES STAGE 3

FIG. 5.3.   *Erection of Yurt, stage 2.*

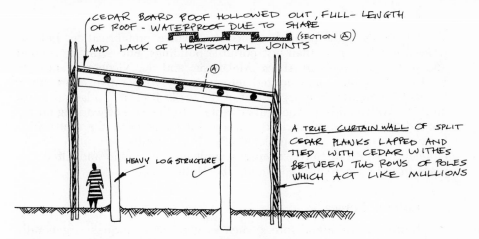

CEDAR BOARD ROOF HOLLOWED OUT, FULL-LENGTH OF ROOF - WATERPROOF DUE TO SHAPE AND LACK OF HORIZONTAL JOINTS

(SECTION Ⓐ)

Ⓐ

HEAVY LOG STRUCTURE

A TRUE CURTAIN WALL OF SPLIT CEDAR PLANKS LAPPED AND TIED WITH CEDAR WITHES BETWEEN TWO ROWS OF POLES WHICH ACT LIKE MULLIONS

FIG. 5.4. *Nootka house, northwest North America.
(Based on models and materials in Peabody Museum at Harvard,
Washington State Museum, and other sources.)*

criteria are optimum use of wood and easy portability on horseback. The solution meets these criteria with walls made up of wooden pantographs the height of a man. These are very light and compact when closed, but open up into sizeable panels. A circle is erected, the plan form of which gives some stability against lateral forces (Fig. 5.2). The roof frame, employing a similar principle, consists of a ring with attached ribs which can be opened easily and placed on top of the wall, relying on its geometry for strength and spanning ability (Fig. 5.3).

The Yurt frame is covered with felt mats which are precut and held down with a traditional pattern of ropes, assuring that as few ropes as possible are used; a Yurt can be erected in half an hour. In the summer one layer of felt and one layer of canvas is used, while in the winter the number of felt layers may go up to eight. Even during 40° below zero weather and howling gales, the Yurt remains warm and comfortable.

The dwellings of the Northwest Indians were also portable, but in a very different way. These dwellings were vast, 25 to 40 feet wide and 60 to 100 feet long,[11] and roofs were either shed or gable, but in either case the structural principle was the same. Timber was the principal material, and there was clear separation between the permanent part of the dwelling—the structure—and the portable part—the sheathing. The structure, of heavy logs, was left in place on the site when the rest of the house was moved, and re-used when needed. Since rivers and other waterways were the routes of transport, the wall and roof boards were not only portable, but, by being lashed across a pair of canoes, provided a platform for goods as well as the materials for a house on the new site (Fig. 5.4).

[11] The Seattle chief lived in a house 900 feet long divided into compartments as needed by matting. See Victor Steinbrueck, *Seattle Cityscape* (Seattle: University of Washington Press, 1962), p. 30.

Prefabrication

Obviously, most portable structures involve prefabrication, but the process involves more than just portable buildings. For example, circular and rectangular roofs in Africa, Melanesia, and the Nicobar Islands are built on the ground and hoisted into place by cooperative effort. Since the roof is structurally independent of the walls, it exerts no lateral thrust on them, which adds a structural advantage to the ease of working on the ground. In other cases, such as Fiji and the Cameroons, the roof grid is built on the ground and completed after being hoisted into place. Walls, either just a grid or fully woven, are built on the ground and tilted into place in the Cameroons and among the Hottentots.

Lateral Forces

Resistance to lateral forces, such as wind or earthquakes, generally requires either rigidity or bracing. An example of a rigid frame is that used in the Northwest Indian house; bracing involves either some form of triangulation, such as trusses, space frames, or buttresses, or shear walls, of which mass structures are one example.

Another way of resisting wind is flexibility, which often depends on the use of tied joints, common in such areas as Malaya and the Cameroons. An occasional refinement, as found among the Bamileke in the Cameroons, is the use of flat strips of bamboo for the tied joints. These grip the cylindrical post much more securely than would round ties, and are self tightening.

The Fiji islands provide a number of examples of methods of dealing with the lateral force problem.[12] In some areas the roofs are very simple

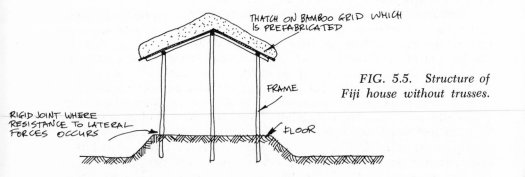

THATCH ON BAMBOO GRID WHICH IS PREFABRICATED

FRAME

FIG. 5.5. Structure of Fiji house without trusses.

RIGID JOINT WHERE RESISTANCE TO LATERAL FORCES OCCURS

FLOOR

and supported by central poles as well as peripheral columns. Since these poles are buried deep in the ground, the building acts as a rigid frame, although the flexibility of the members themselves assures some flexibility (Fig. 5.5). In other parts of the islands roofs consist of trusses made by tying the members together. Overhangs are not used in order to avoid

[12] Based on information given by Professor Fritz Janeba, now at the *Akademie für Angewandte Kunst* in Vienna.

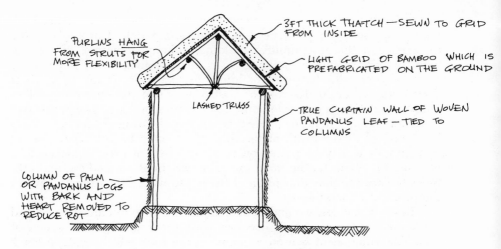

FIG. 5.6. *Fiji house with trusses.*

the uplift in the strong winds and storms common to the area. The frame of the house is not triangulated, so in case of a hurricane the structure sways and gives, much like a palm tree. Should the house collapse, the roof, being braced, usually remains in one piece on the ground and provides shelter from the heavy rains which accompany the storms (Fig. 5.6). This is far more efficient, and safer, than the corrugated iron roofs, which tend to blow off sheet by sheet.

Weathering

A 1959 English study pointed out that traditional building has taken into account the forces of climate, aspect, site, height of building, and severity of exposure as they affect weathering, and that modern builders need to consider these forces carefully since they lack intimate knowledge of local conditions.[13] It might be added that consideration of weathering, as well as appropriate use of materials and their jointing, has often been neglected in modern buildings. The great choice of materials has freed builders from former limitations, one immediate result being the bad weathering of buildings. New materials are used thoughtlessly, without due attention to their characteristics and in ignorance of exposure conditions. The respect of primitive and vernacular builders for the innate qualities and characteristics of materials is worthy of study, since they accept constraints and treat the influence of time and weather as allies rather than enemies. Sun is used to cure adobe and mud; rain is used to harden hydraulic cement; the absorption and evaporation of moisture by thatch helps avoid condensation problems. Materials are selected not only in terms of their adequacy for structure, tooling, laying, and jointing, but also with a view to the impact of time.

[13] Department of Scientific and Industrial Research, *Principles of Modern Building*, 3rd ed. (London: HMSO, 1959), Vol. I, pp. 81-82.

Concern with the time dimension is due to the direct feedback already discussed, and to the need to conserve materials. This applies more to vernacular than to primitive building, although examples of concern with the performance of buildings over time are found even in primitive cultures. Generally, however, buildings in such cultures are fairly short lived, and are often deserted or destroyed when the owner dies. This temporal relation of owner to house is a complex problem. The house may be temporary and replaced many times during the owner's lifetime; it may be destroyed at the death of the owner; [14] it may be left vacant to fall into ruin, or it may be passed on to his children; it may be moved to a new site or rebuilt on the same site. The variations are endless, and attitudes toward the time dimension of the house will affect attitudes toward the problem of weathering.

In the Cyclades, we find dependence on nature to cure the puddled earth (patelia) roof, which becomes waterproof through the action of rain. The same agent is used to maintain the roof, which tends to crack during the dry season. Before the first rains a layer of dry earth is placed on the roof; they wash this dirt into the cracks, which are thus sealed.[15] A similar method is used among the Pueblos. The form of roof boards in the Northwest Indian house has as much to do with weathering as with initial watertightness.

Great care is taken in some areas to cure timber adequately and then leave it unpainted so that it can "breathe." Various special protective coatings may be used, such as the mixture of soot and persimmon juice in Japan, and the rust and skim milk of the American barn. In Japan wood is sometimes carbonized for protection, while shingles in the United States were cured by immersion in salt water for several weeks. There are instances where they have proved more durable than three sets of nails.[16] To protect them from rot, timber posts are often placed on stones, as in Japan, or on pads of "concrete" which, in Malaya, are made of a mixture of limestone, crushed sea shells, and honey.

In Vera Cruz, Mexico, thatched roofs are carefully shaped and woven, and a single ridge point and steep pitch spread the water to all four sides of the roof. Flashing of long rice straw is used to waterproof the four ridges. The straw hangs from the projecting eaves throwing the water clear of the split bamboo walls. The house remains waterproof and well ventilated no matter how hard it rains.[17]

The Kikuyu dwelling in Africa has mud walls, either because of climate or of retention of a dry weather type of construction in the move to a rainy area, with the consequent problem of protecting them from

---

[14] See Deffontaines, *Géographie et Religions,* pp. 33-38, for the impact of the attitude toward the dead on the duration of the house. See also Mircea Eliade, *The Sacred and the Profane* (New York: Harper & Row, 1961), p. 57.

[15] C. Papas, *L'Urbanisme et l'Architecture Populaire dans les Cyclades* (Paris: Editions Dunod, 1957), p. 140.

[16] For Japan, see Taut, *Houses and People of Japan,* p. 74; for American examples, see Sibyl Moholy-Nagy, *Native Genius in Anonymous Architecture* (New York: Horizon Press, 1957), p. 192.

[17] Moholy-Nagy, *Native Genius in Anonymous Architecture,* p. 94.

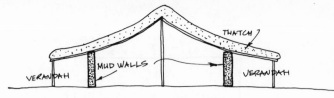

FIG. 5.7. *Kikuyu house.*

the rain. Protection is given by a wide verandah, a fairly common solution to the problem in a number of areas (Fig. 5.7).

I have already discussed the use of double walls and roofs of leaves and thatch in Africa and India to protect mud construction from the rain, as well as for climatic reasons. Use in the Congo of a layer of leaves to protect thatch would seem to indicate a deliberate attempt to protect the main layer from drying out and cracking in the sun, since there seems to be no climatic advantage to the double layer. The thatched roof is carefully constructed of leaves which act much like shingles or tiles, and which, in their shape and pattern, resemble the scales of an animal called a pangolin (Fig. 5.8). (The natives believe that they received this method

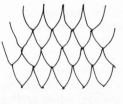

MAIN ROOF OF LEAVES LIKE
THE SCALES OF THE
PANGOLIN

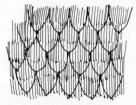

LAYER OF BRANCHES
OVER THE MAIN ROOF

FIG. 5.8. *Congo roof.*

of roofing from the animal.) On top of this thatch are placed branches and narrow leaves which turn yellow and dry while the main roof remains green and waterproof in the heavy rains. Tests in a number of areas have shown that thatched roofs are often more waterproof than many army tents.

The Massa in the Cameroons use a more formalized version of the same principle in which two thatched roofs are placed one over the other (Fig. 5.9). A similar device was used in early Canada, where the thick

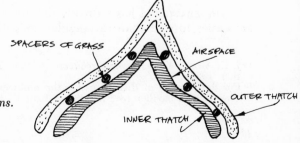

FIG. 5.9. *Massa roof, Cameroons.*

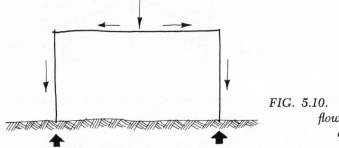

FIG. 5.10. *Diagram showing flow of forces through a structural frame.*

rubble walls, while successful against heat and cold and possessing structural stability, deteriorated seriously because of the alternate frosts and thaws of winter. These walls, particularly the exposed east and north faces, were then covered with boarding, which kept the stone dry and thus immune to frost.[18]

Gravity

In order to handle the problem of gravity, any structure needs two components—a horizontally spanning element which collects the forces, and a vertical component which carries them to the ground, where they can be resisted (Fig. 5.10).[19] Without going into structural theory, it is intuitively clear that the major problem involves the horizontally spanning element, which is the one that encloses space, and that the character of this element will have a major effect on the form of the dwelling. In single story dwellings (and we are primarily discussing this type), this element is the *roof*, which has, in fact, often been used as the principal element of house form classification.

PURE TENSILE STRUCTURES.   Any member which is to span space needs tensile strength. One approach to this spanning problem uses the great effectiveness of certain materials in tension to produce efficient, light structures with little material. One striking example is the Arab tent, where slender poles stuck in the ground, the vertical elements, form a demountable framework and are joined by a light, tensile membrane of felt, goatskin, or calfskin which is both structure and enclosure (Fig. 5.11). This is a sophisticated structure of great efficiency, and variations of it are found in other areas. It is also in the news today as the basis of a new structural method for large buildings.[20]

THE FRAME.   I have already discussed the argument that round huts are easier to roof than rectangular ones, have suggested that there may

---

[18] J. E. Aronin, *Climate and Architecture* (New York: Reinhold Publishing Corporation, 1953), p. 7.
[19] For the purpose of this discussion the problem of lateral forces is neglected.
[20] The German pavilion by Frei Otto at Expo 67 in Montreal is an example.

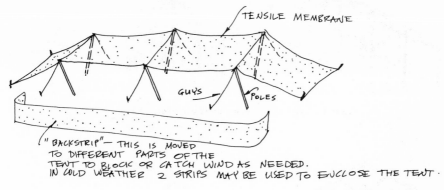

TENSILE MEMBRANE

GUYS

POLES

"BACKSTRIP"— THIS IS MOVED
TO DIFFERENT PARTS OF THE
TENT TO BLOCK OR CATCH WIND AS NEEDED.
IN COLD WEATHER 2 STRIPS MAY BE USED TO ENCLOSE THE TENT.

FIG. 5.11. Arab tent.

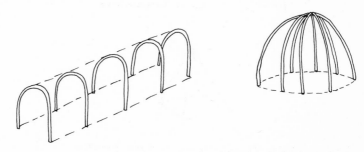

FIG. 5.12. Hoop structures—rectangular and circular plan.

be symbolic reasons for the distinction, and have also pointed out that both types coexist in a number of cultures.[21] The problem concerning the frame in terms of construction is the *span*. For small spans, rectangular and circular shapes hold equal difficulty; in the simplest case, hoops can be used for both types (Fig. 5.12). Once the span increases, two procedures are possible. The first is to introduce internal supports, while the other is to use some form of truss (Fig. 5.13). In either case, there is implicit need for materials with some tensile strength, such as timber.

We can see that the principle and problem are the same whether the dwelling is rectangular or round, but since this distinction has been used extensively, it provides a reasonable framework for discussion.

Round dwellings. These range from small one-man huts to houses 60 feet and more in diameter, and are found among South American Indians, in Indonesia, Lapland, and above all in Africa. The simplest is the dwelling with a structure of a series of hoops thatched with leaves (Fig. 5.14). In some cases the ribs may be tied at the top rather than forming

---

[21] Stuart Piggott, ed., *The Dawn of Civilization* (London: Thames and Hudson, 1961), illustrations, pp. 100-101. In Upper Egypt, in Amratian times (*ca.* 3800 B.C.) we find rectangular huts for the two sacred personages—the chief, who was also the medicine man, and the rainmaker; and beehive-shaped round huts in the rest of the village. There are similar examples from many other cultures and times.

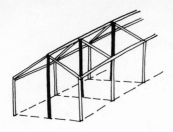

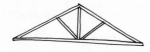 CENTRAL POSTS (ONE DIMENSIONAL)

TRUSSES (TWO DIMENSIONAL)

SPACE FRAME (THREE DIMENSIONAL)

FIG. 5.13. Three ways of handling increased roof spans.

FIG. 5.14. Bakinga Pygmy hut.

FIG. 5.15. Kenya hut.

FRAMEWORK

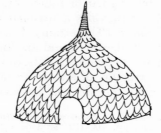

COVERING

hoops, but they also form a skeleton covered by thatch (Fig. 5.15). In other cases the walls may be woven like a basket for greater rigidity, and mats placed over them can be moved as the wind changes (Fig. 5.16).

The ribs may also be supported by a separate wall, as in the Mongol Yurt, and as we find in Africa and the Marquesas (Fig. 5.17). When the dwelling increases in size, a central pole may be needed to support the roof at the apex (Fig. 5.18). Alternatively, this support can be given by a space frame, which is a rather sophisticated device and has the advantage of freeing the floor (Fig. 5.19).

In all these cases the walls may be of any material—leaves, clay, grass, mats—since they are true curtain walls; the choice may depend on tradition, climate, or, in some cases, the inability of hoops to carry heavy loads.

The tepee of the North American Indians is partly a space frame, and uses a tensile membrane, which makes it a link between the frame

FIG. 5.16.
Khoisan hut, South Africa.

FIG. 5.17.   Framework of Marquesas dwelling.

FIG. 5.18.   Framework of Waiwai dwelling in Guyana (South America).

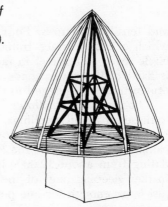

FIG. 5.19.   Space frame support, Bamileke, Cameroons.
(Adapted from Beguin, Kalt et al., L'habitat au Cameroun, p. 76.)

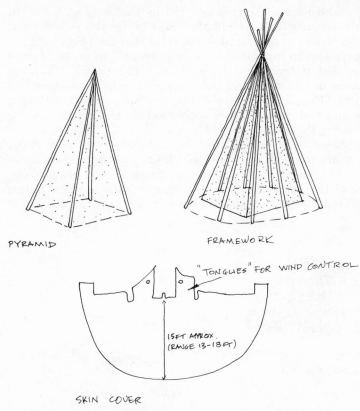

PYRAMID

FRAMEWORK

"TONGUES" FOR WIND CONTROL

15FT APPROX.
(RANGE 13-18FT)

SKIN COVER

FIG. 5.20. *Plains Indians' tepee.*

FIG. 5.21.
"Sleeping bag," Sepik River.

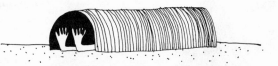

and tensile structures. Four poles are first erected to form a pyramid, which acts as a space frame, and then about half a dozen ribs form a circle seven to ten feet in radius and 16 feet high. The last of these ribs is fixed to the cover, made of a dozen or more buffalo hides, which is drawn tight and pegged to the ground (Fig. 5.20).

Rectangular dwellings. The solutions in this case are very similar to those for round dwellings. In the simplest examples hoops are also used, but arranged in line to produce a rectangular plan. This ancient form can be seen sketched in the *Font de Gaume* caves in southwestern France dating from about 12,000–10,000 B.C. The hoops can be very small, as in the "sleeping bag" of the Sepik River area of New Guinea, which is just large enough for one person to slide into (Fig. 5.21). They can also

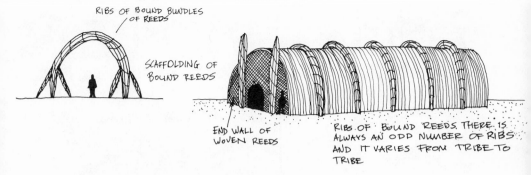

FIG. 5.22. Marsh Arabs. Left: Erection of ribs. Right: Meeting hall.

reach large sizes, as, for example, among the marsh dwellers of Iraq, near the Iranian border, where reeds are the only materials available and everything is built of them—the ribs, the sheathing, and the scaffolding used during construction (Fig. 5.22).

The size of such large buildings, consisting of a series of hoops covered with such light materials as mats, bamboo, leaves, reeds, or thatch, is limited by the height of the ribs since they cannot take much lateral pressure. This problem is overcome by using heavier timber for wall and roof members, but as soon as the span gets at all large, problems are created. The simplest solution is to support the ridge with a series of uprights at the center of the dwelling, as shown in Figure 5.13. This form is similar whether it is prehistoric or recent, in Melanesia, Polynesia, Africa, South India, Malaya, or tropical America, and on the ground or on stilts above it. It can be covered with any material desired, and is, in principle, very similar to many houses built in the United States today.

In order to dispense with the central row of uprights, a roof consisting of trusses is needed. This is found in Malaya, Fiji, and other areas, but was not really common before the coming of vernacular building. This is a "carpenter's" roof, usually requiring tradesmen, and is typical of most peasant cultures.[22] Alternatively, a three-dimensional truss—a space frame—can be used, very similar to those already described for round dwellings.[23]

The vernacular tradition displays very few devices not found in primitive buildings. The sophistication of joints and trusses becomes greater, as in the medieval house, houses may have more than one story, and the framing details get more complex, as in the carpenter frame of

[22] For some examples see Richard Weiss, *Häuser und Landschaften der Schweiz* (Erlenbach-Zurich: Eugen Rentsch Verlag, 1959); B. I. Stoianov, *Starata Rodopska Architektura* (The Old Architecture of the Rhodope [Bulgaria]) (Sofia: Techkniga, 1964); Smialkowski, *Architektura i Budownictwo Pasterskie w Tatrach Polskich* (Architecture and Construction of Shepherds' Buildings in the Polish Tatras) (Kracow: Government Scientific Publishing House, 1959); Werner Radig, *Frühformen der Hausentwicklung in Deutschland* (Berlin: Hanschel Verlag, 1958).
[23] See Amos Rapoport, "Yagua, or the Amazon Dwelling," *Landscape*, XVI, No. 3 (Spring 1967), 27-30.

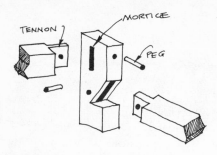

FIG. 5.23.   Carpenter frame.

FIG. 5.24.   Corbelled vault.

early Arkansas, used prior to the 1840's. Similar framing, with notched timbers, was also used in New England barns. Pegs were sometimes inserted in a "draw bore" where the dowel hole was sufficiently askew to make the entire assembly rigid when the peg was inserted (Fig. 5.23).

One of the few new developments is the balloon frame of the United States, which is related to the development of industrial processes. It is also linked to the growing use of carpenters, as differentiation of trades progresses and the specialist builder is able to do things that cannot be done by the average person.

COMPRESSION.   In areas where stone and mud alone are used, either because materials with any degree of tensile strength are not available, or are not utilized for various reasons, another way of spanning space, which relies on materials in compression, must be used. Under these conditions, neither the one- nor two-dimensional forms of structure will work for creating usable spaces, and construction must be of the three-dimensional type, which does its job through its geometry. This implies the use of some form of arch, vault, or dome, although use of this form is not fully determined by the material. We have seen arched forms constructed with timber and reeds—materials strong in tension.

There are various forms of corbelled vaults or domes. Some, involving dry construction without mortar, such as the "borie" of the Celtic civilization, which were still being built in Provence in the eighteenth century, work by *pure* compression, while those with mortar have some small tensile strength. The latter type were used in Mycenean times, among the Mayas, and in Iran, Iceland, Italy, Peru, South Africa, and Turkey. While the specific forms may be very different, they all rely on the same principle, with each stone or brick projecting beyond the one below it (Fig. 5.24).

The true dome and vault, or systems of vaults and domes, are found in many areas of the Middle East. A refinement of the dome is the

FIG. 5.25.   *Doubly curved mud-vault roof, Iran.*

Eskimo Igloo, with its spiral coursing, while a refinement of the vault is the doubly curved shell of Iran, which gains strength and stiffness by being curved in different directions (Fig. 5.25). In the Gorfa villages of the Sahara, the shell-roofed units are combined in the form of a honey-comb for strength.

The effect of these structural systems on house form is obvious. They also influence the form of the plan because they exert considerable lateral thrust. This leads to the use of thick walls, buttresses, and so on. Since spans are also limited, spaces tend to be small and buildings tend to be aggregates of units rather than divisions within an over-all shell. However, as we have seen, this is also a cultural distinction independent of structure and material.

VERTICAL LOAD-CARRYING ELEMENTS.   Vertical load-carrying elements, which collect the forces from the spanning members and transfer them to the ground, present a distinction similar to that between three-dimensional and other structures. The choice is between frames consisting of columns, which need enclosure for weather and privacy in the form of curtain walls, or bearing walls, which are both structure and enclosure. In either case there is a limitation in the amount of area which they can take up, both in plan and in section, in order to provide usable living space (Fig. 5.26).

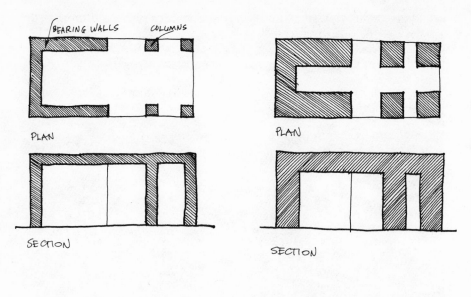

FIG. 5.26. *Vertical load-carrying elements.*

INHERENTLY UNSTABLE   INHERENTLY STABLE

FIG. 5.27. *The geometry of bearing walls and stability.*

The decision as to whether columns or frames are to be used seems to depend on tradition, the materials chosen (largely those strong in compression—stone, adobe, and timber), climate, and so on. It seems difficult to attribute the choice to any simple, utilitarian factor. Columns and bearing walls are relatively simple in concept, and their use is limited largely by their tendency to buckle, which restricts the height for any given thickness. This can lead to very massive elements. In order to reduce the bulk of walls, they need to be reinforced with buttresses or piers, or need changes in plane with reentry corners, which adds to their three-dimensional quality, and hence their stability. Both buttresses and changes of plane affect the plan form, and lead to a whole set of form consequences through the use of niches, recesses, and modelling of the surface through the casting of shadows (Fig. 5.27). This can become the earmark of a whole way of building, vernacular as well as high-style.[24]

[24] Amos Rapoport, "The Architecture of Isphahan," *Landscape*, XIV, No. 2 (Winter 1964-65), 4-11.

Many devices of great ingenuity and sophistication are used in the construction of bearing walls. Pueblo walls are built much like concrete walls today; tall buildings were constructed in the Arabian desert and the Atlas mountains of Southern Morocco; reinforcing fibers and armatures were used in mud walls in primitive cultures of Africa and South America, a development parallelled by the complex half-timbering in the vernacular context, which needs the special skills of the carpenter; heavy log walls are found from Scandinavia through Poland, Siberia, and Nepal, all the way to Japan, were brought to the United States, and are all remarkably uniform in type, with ingenious jointing methods at the corners. All of these have relatively little effect on the form of the dwelling; it is the decision to use logs rather than frame and cover, or adobe rather than something else, which is important. What all these variations show is the great choice possible, and the relatively low criticality of building constructions.

CHAPTER 6   *a look at the present*

We have seen that some of the dominant characteristics of primitive and vernacular building lose force with the greater institutionalization and specialization of modern life. Our different view of time, involving a strong sense of its linearity, progress, and historicity, replaces the more cyclic time concepts of primitive man. As a result modern man, particularly in the United States, stresses change and novelty as being of the essence—a very different situation from that prevailing under the conditions we have been discussing. The clear hierarchy of primitive and vernacular settlements is lost, reflecting the general loss of hierarchies within society, and all buildings tend to have equal prominence. The desanctification of nature has led to the dehumanization of our relationship with the land and the site. Modern man has lost the mythological and cosmological orientation which was so important to primitive man, or has substituted new mythologies in place of the old. He has also lost the shared image of the good life and its values, unless he can be said to have the shared image of *no* image. Forces and pressures are also much more complex, and the links among form, culture, and behavior are more tenuous, or possibly just more difficult to trace and establish.[1]

In view of all this, the following question remains to be considered: To what extent does the conceptual framework proposed apply to house form today? If this framework can still be applied today, it will not only explain the past but also illuminate the future. The difference between high-style and popular building still exists, and applies to houses as well as to the roadside architecture. It is the tract house rather than the archi-

---

[1] The latter is probably the case. I explored this subject in a graduate seminar at the University of California, Berkeley, and it was clear that the world view is still dominant in the formation of landscapes, cities, buildings, and house form.

tect designed house that needs to be discussed in order to discover which of the values it represents might help explain its success.

I am adopting the view that there is some difference between the two types of building, in spite of Dwight MacDonald's argument that the distinction between high culture and folk culture no longer exists. If we consider architect designed buildings as high-style, and primitive and vernacular buildings as folk art, then, following his argument, modern nonarchitect designed buildings should belong to what he calls "masscult." While folk art is created *by* the people when there is community, masscult comes from above *to* the people when there is a mass —atomized man. His examples are mostly from music—comparing jazz and popular music—and literature, but apply equally well to roadside architecture and tract houses.[2] These roadside and tract buildings represent certain values which are lacking in architect designed buildings, and which tell us something about life-styles, thus explaining their acceptance and commercial success. Even though people no longer build their own houses, the houses they buy reflect popular values and goals more closely than do those of the design subculture—and these houses constitute the bulk of the built environment.[3]

This difference between the popular and the architect designed house can still help us gain an insight into the needs, values, and desires of people. Modern man may still have his own myths, and the forms of houses, while very different in their specifics, may be due to motivations not inherently different from those of the past, and still primarily socio-cultural in the sense that I have proposed. Differences among the built environments of the United States, France, and England can be understood in terms of laissez-faire, open ended, process oriented American attitude, the French urban tradition, which affects not just the town but also the rural landscape with "urban" qualities, and the "anti-urban" tradition of England, which helps explain the character of many urban areas in that country. There is still, therefore, the old search for the ideal environment of which the house is merely one physical embodiment, and the recent tendency in the United States to design housing estates and "new towns" around recreational facilities is a striking reflection of an old ideal in a new guise.[4]

A few examples will show that forms still reflect the old concerns. It has been pointed out that a great deal can be discovered about a legal

---

[2] Dwight MacDonald, *Against the American Grain* (New York: Random House, Inc., 1962), pp. 3-75. According to him, masscult starts in the eighteenth century, and whereas folk art parallels high culture, masscult *competes* with it. I would add that this is the difference between participants and consumers. John Kouwenhoeven, in *The Beercan by the Highway* (Garden City, N.Y.: Doubleday and Co., 1961), and other writings, implicitly disagrees with MacDonald, suggesting that there is a vital American vernacular.

[3] During the graduate seminar already referred to, we compared values attached to houses in the popular press and in the architectural journals, and found that they discussed and praised totally different sets of criteria.

[4] With reference to high-style buildings, the primacy of socio-cultural factors can also be seen clearly. We can trace it historically in the work of Emile Mâle on Gothic; Rudolf Wittkower on the Renaissance; Banham, Collins, and others on the modern movement.

system by noting the way courtroom furniture is arranged. This can tell us the position of the defendant and how he is treated, the relative power of prosecutor and defending attorney, and so on.[5] Similarly, the arrangements possible between just two chairs in a psychotherapy session are remarkably indicative of the roles of the people involved and the values and goals of the particular school of psychotherapy; the same implications can be noted for larger groupings of seats, such as the dining counter in America.[6] This can also apply to other buildings, and the comment has been made that the design of mental hospitals tells more about the people who design, build, and maintain them than about the people incarcerated in them.[7]

All of this evidence suggests the close relation still prevailing between culture and form. The danger of ignoring it is brought out by a lawyer's complaint that, in the design of new courthouses, architects, in their search for minimum circulation (one of their currently held values) have neglected the importance of the corridor for informal deals and conferences. He claims that this is seriously interfering with the administration of justice.[8]

Developing Countries

Many aspects could be discussed before looking at the forces which may possibly shape the popular house in our culture, but I will briefly mention only one—the problem of developing countries. One characteristic of such countries is often the breakdown of folk arts, which cease to have symbolic value and hence no longer communicate. This may well be related to the need to limit language for purposes of communication, which involves the important question of choice. The problem today seems to be one of excessive choice, and the breakdown of folk art may be due to the fact that the vocabulary is not limited and choice becomes too difficult. Folk art would then be seen not as the result of some mysterious good taste, but as the result of learning to make choices among a limited number of approved alternatives. It is interesting to observe the contrast between choices of traditional and new artifacts in Japan, between traditional and new textiles in Mexico, or traditional and new music in India; the lack of "taste" shown with reference to new products and buildings may merely be an inability to choose outside the framework of traditional forms.

The topic of choice may be relevant to other aspects of developing countries, and may throw light on the whole problem of understanding

---

[5] John N. Hazard, "Furniture Arrangements as a Symbol of Judicial Roles," *ETC: A Review of General Semantics*, XIX, No. 2 (July 1962), 181-188.

[6] See Paul Goodman, "The Meaning of Functionalism," *Journal of Architectural Education*, XIV, No. 2 (Autumn 1959), 32-38.

[7] See Humphrey Osmond in *Who Designs America?*, ed. L. B. Holland (Garden City, N.Y.: Doubleday and Co., 1966), p. 287. See also Osmond's work on seating arrangements in geriatrics wards and evidence from the work of E. T. Hall, Robert Sommer, Abraham Maslow, and others.

[8] Letter to the Editor, *The New York Times*, August 1, 1966, p. 26.

the relation of built form to the cultures concerned, in turn making clear the value of cross-cultural analysis in relation to the house and built environment in general. There is a danger in applying Western concepts, which represent only one choice among the many possible, to the problems of other areas, instead of looking at them in terms of local way of life, specific needs, and ways of doing things. A minor example is the problem, encountered in Rangoon and Bangkok, of providing little abodes for the guardian spirits of each house in the context of the multifamily high-rise dwelling.[9] One could say that the need is unreasonable, but we have already seen that neglect of traditional cultural patterns may have serious results.

Charles Abrams was one of the first to realize this point and to deal with it in connection with built environment and the house. He has often commented in his work on how experts and officials deplore traditional solutions in spite of their clear social and climatic advantages. He refers to the adoption, in Ghana, of the English slogan "one family—one house," and points out that the family in Ghana is something very different, and its relation to the house not the same,[10] a clear instance of the importance of dealing with the *specifics* of the situation.

All housing needs to achieve four objectives in order to be successful:

1. It needs to be socially and culturally valid.
   (Here traditional housing possibly works best.)
2. It should be sufficiently economical to ensure that the greatest number can afford it.
   (In primitive and vernacular contexts most, if not all, people have houses.)
3. It should ensure the maintenance of the health of the occupants.
   (In relation to climate traditional housing succeeds, in relation to sanitation and parasites it usually fails.)
4. There should be a minimum of maintenance over the life of the building.
   (Here the evidence is equivocal.)

If we accept that the utilitarian functions of the house are not primary, and at the same time realize that even those functions may be better satisfied by traditional housing than by new housing in many areas, our attitude toward traditional housing may change.

Traditional housing may therefore be much more acceptable—if not, in fact, desirable—than has been assumed, and housing attitudes in developing countries should possibly be adjusted accordingly. At the very least this offers a fruitful field for research.

Examples of the nonutilitarian values which we have encountered in economies of scarcity still prevail in the barriadas of Peru, and, no

---

[9] On Bangkok, see *The New York Times*, July 24, 1967, p. 16, which points out that every plot of ground has its spirit, and building a house would drive it away and bring misfortune. On Rangoon see Gerald Breese, *Urbanization in Newly Developing Countries* (Englewood Cliffs, N.J.: Prentice-Hall, Inc., 1966), pp. 98-99.

[10] The Ghanese women traditionally live apart from the men and share a communal kitchen. When one was asked whether she would like to live in a house with her husband, she pointed out that he had five other wives, only gave her £1 a week, and that she was very happy to spend only part of the time with him. Abrams asks why an alien pattern should be imposed on her.

doubt, in other similar areas. It has been reported [11] that when the walls of a house in the barriada are finished, the rooms are usually roofed with cane, the windows bricked up, and cement floors put in. With the first money earned after the walls are paid for, a large, elaborate cedar door (costing about $45) is purchased. Upon installation of this door and wooden windows, the people feel like owners. In the example cited, the concrete roof was not started until two years later, after a damp winter when the children became ill. Thus even in barriada the status symbol of the house—the door—takes precedence over the utility of keeping out rain and cold. Many houses may also have the facade and a "parlor" finished to "quite high standards and considerable expense before the rest of the dwelling is complete." [12]

In East Pakistan, where the severe climate imposes many constraints on house form, and poverty is very great, the relation of such elements as toilets and beds to Mecca (East) is regarded as equally as critical as climate and economy.[13] No doubt examples could be multiplied, but the point is clear, and Americans and Englishmen are no different.

The Case of Our Own Culture

Let us turn to the Western world, and see whether the basic framework suggested helps us in any way to understand the form of the popular house.

The prevalent attitude toward planning and design in the United States makes the norm the white, middle-class family of parents and two children typified by advertising. This leaves out millions who have different values and do not fit this package, even though these subcultural differences are of great importance. Consider, for example, the way working-class people use part of the settlement—the neighborhood—in a manner much more closely related to the Mediterranean tradition than to the Anglo-American one.[14] This will have, or *should* have, profound effects on the image and form of the house and settlement, and is a distinction I have already discussed with regard to England.

Definition of the image and meaning of the house is of great importance; it can help explain the difference between houses on the East Coast and California, and can be an important aspect in low-cost housing. For example, agricultural workers in the Central valley of California,

---

[11] William Mangin, "Urbanization Case History in Peru," *Architectural Design* (London), XXXIII (August 1963), 369.

[12] John C. Turner, "Barriers and Channels for Housing Development in Modernizing Countries," *Journal of the AIP*, XXXIII, No. 3 (May 1967), 179.

[13] Lecture at the Department of Architecture, University of California, Berkeley, April 18, 1967, by Stanley Tigerman of Chicago.

[14] See Marc Fried, "Functions of Working Class Community in Modern Urban Society: Implications for Forced Relocation," *Journal of the AIP*, XXXIII, No. 2 (March 1967), 90 ff., especially 92, 100, and references on 102; see also Marc Fried, "Grieving for a Lost Home," in *The Urban Condition*, ed. Leonard Duhl.

in self-help housing, build "ranchhouses" based on the popular press image, a symbol of belonging through the middle-class house. These people are not confident enough to be different, to express their own traditions, or even to respond directly to the needs of the area. It may well be that the expression of subcultural traditions is more likely in areas such as Latin America, Africa, and Asia, where these cultures are stronger than among, say, Mexican-Americans.[15]

Within the middle-class culture itself, dwelling forms change to accommodate people outside the "standard family" through new types of popular housing. An example is the recent development of a new type of apartment for single people in cities.[16] I have already suggested (in Chapter 1) that the vernacular today may be one of *type* rather than of form. This particular type came from the needs of a specific group, felt by an entrepreneur; the need was real, as shown by the great success of his efforts. The new social role this housing fills has strong form consequences in the stress placed on communal and recreational facilities, and the way in which spaces are used to fulfill this new role.

Turning to the single family house and its parts, there is still a link between behavioral patterns and form.

Consider the impact of attitudes toward eating, for example, on house form. It makes a major difference whether one has a formal family meal in a separate dining room or eats in the kitchen; whether everyone eats separately whenever he wishes or all eat together; or whether one eats indoors at all. The prevalence of the barbecue in Los Angeles affects more than just house form, since increasing use of the backyard, with its barbecue and swimming pool, makes it, and the house, more than ever the center of life. Patterns of formality or informality in dining still play an important role in molding childhood attitudes, and to that extent the house is still a mechanism for shaping character.

Attitudes toward the bathroom in the United States, which enabled Miner to write the brilliant paper to which I referred in Chapter 1, are largely cultural. A recent major study of the topic shows clearly that the form of the bathroom is the result of attitudes about the body, relaxation, privacy, and so on.[17] It has frequently been observed by visitors that American houses are advertised by the number of bathrooms they possess, which often exceeds the number of bedrooms. This brings us back to the problem of *basic needs*. The same fundamental problems of hygiene have always existed, but the importance attached to them, and the forms used, have been very different, depending on beliefs, fears,

---

[15] Even in the United States one can find examples of the expression of cultural differences. A student of mine—Mr. Edward Long—found that Mexican and Japanese neighborhoods in Los Angeles, which began with identical houses, took on very different characteristics because of the symbolism of the landscaping. (This is my interpretation, not his; he was concerned with a different aspect of the problem.)

[16] *Time*, LXXXVIII, No. 9 (August 26, 1966), p. 49.

[17] Alexander Kira, *The Bathroom* (Ithaca, N.Y.: Cornell University Center for Housing and Environmental Studies, Research Report No. 7, 1966). It is interesting that most reviewers stressed the physical, rather than the cultural and psychological, aspects of the study.

and values rather than utilitarian considerations. For example, the choice between tub and shower is largely a matter of attitudes and images.[18]

In the same way, attitudes toward privacy are still very much culturally shaped, and have great impact on house form. These attitudes not only differ between Germany and the United States, and even England and the United States,[19] but also among different subcultures in this country. This may be why the "open plan," so beloved of the architect, has never really been accepted by the public. With regard to noise, we can contrast the Italian tolerance, even love, of noise with the German abhorrence of it.[20] It has also been pointed out that in Europe the stress is more on "gracious living" than on gadgets, and that standards of sound insulation are consequently much higher than in the United States, where economic considerations are more important in spite of the greater wealth.[21] Concern with noise in this country began with a 1948 lawsuit against a company for loss of hearing,[22] which supports the view that in America the prevalence of insurance lawsuits and the consequent search for safety become an important form determinant.[23] It can also be shown that the attitudes of lending agencies, tax policies, and government regulations of all sorts, such as codes and zoning, are all important sociocultural form determinants which reflect the values and ethos of the society.

It may be that the modern house orients itself to the view, beach, sun, and sky, and that this orientation, and the picture window, replace the religious, symbolic orientation of the past. Therefore, a new symbol takes over—health, sun, and sport *as an idea*. We could say that in the United States the ideal of health becomes a new religion.[24]

What then does "house" mean to Americans? They have a dream "home—the very word can reduce my compatriots to tears,"[25] and builders and developers never build houses, they build homes. The dream home is surrounded by trees and grass in either country or suburb, and must be *owned*, yet Americans rarely stay in it more than 5 years. It is not a real need but a symbol.

---

[18] *Ibid.*, pp. 8-10.
[19] E. T. Hall, *The Hidden Dimension* (Garden City, N.Y.: Doubleday and Co., 1966), pp. 123-137.
[20] E. T. Hall, lecture at the University of California, Winter Quarter, 1967.
[21] Leo L. Baranek, "Noise," *Scientific American*, CCXV, No. 6 (December 1966), 72. As a non-American, I must also comment on the great tolerance of Americans to noise on which I, and many visitors, have remarked; and on the difference in attitudes to noise and privacy between the United States and Australia.
[22] *Ibid.*, p. 66.
[23] Boris Pushkarev, "Scale and Design in a New Environment," in *Who Designs America?*, ed. L. B. Holland, pp. 113-115.
[24] See H. G. West, "The House is a Compass," *Landscape*, I, No. 2 (Autumn 1951), 24-27. This topic has been studied by J. B. Jackson. He suggested this view to me in personal conversation and also during a seminar at the Department of Landscape Architecture, University of California, Berkeley, Winter 1967; see also his "The Westward Moving House," *Landscape*, II, No. 3 (Spring 1953), 8-21, on how three attitudes toward life in the United States produced three different types of house.
[25] John Steinbeck, "Fact and Fancy," *San Francisco Examiner*, March 30, 1967.

This symbol means a freestanding, single family house, *not* a row house, and the ideal of home is aesthetic, not functional.[26] In a recent advertisement showing 49 new uses of aluminum in a house, the form of the house is colonial—the symbol of home to many Americans even in a twentieth century material.[27] The symbol is not necessarily good or reasonable in terms of utility, and has, in fact, been criticized, but it is real and represents a world view and an ethos. This becomes particularly clear if the American attitude is compared with a study in Vienna, where 61 per cent of the people wanted apartments in the center of town, 51 per cent preferred multistory buildings, and other preferences were equally different from the prevailing American attitude.[28]

The whole concept of the private house and the fence may well be an expression of territoriality, which seems to be a crucial concept, although it can take on different forms. The nature of territorial symbols in relation to problems of overpopulation, crowding, and so on, is a matter of great importance.[29]

The impact of ideas and attitudes on basic needs and symbols of privacy is striking. I have already referred to the two types of humanism in architecture, and the implication that in the United States utility (and one might add, novelty) has become essential. Yet it could be asked whether it is utility or the idea of utility—the image it represents—which is sought. The success of the Rossmoor development, which differs from other subdivisions primarily by being walled, has been attributed to that wall around it which ". . . made a big difference. People responded to the idea of the enclosed community—a symbol of security and prestige." [30] The ideal of prestige can become a vital consideration in selection of house sites today, as shown by the idea of the "wrong side of the tracks" and the notion of "fashionable" areas. The way these locations change within one city, depending on social rather than physical factors, is revealing, as is the whole phenomenon of changing fashions in towns and areas of towns. In general, one could argue that modern symbols related to the house are as strong as those of the past, and still take precedence over physical aspects—they are only different.

As one example, consider the fence. Visitors from Australia and England are struck by the lack of fences in American suburbs, and find it difficult to understand. The front fence in those other countries gives no real visual or acoustic privacy, but symbolizes a frontier and barrier. A British fence manufacturer is quoted as saying, ". . . it's man putting

---

[26] See Richard D. Cramer, "Images of Home," *AIA Journal*, XLVI, No. 3 (September 1960), 41, 44; also "The Builder's Architect," *Architectural Forum*, XCV, No. 6 (December 1951), 118-125, which discusses public house preferences in the tract house field. It is clear that these preferences are symbolic.

[27] Reynolds Aluminum Company advertisement, *Time*, LXXXIX, No. 18 (May 5, 1967), pp. 92-93.

[28] Cited in *Landscape*, VII, No. 2 (Winter 1957-58), 2.

[29] The work of the ethologists, such as Calhoun, Christian, Lorentz, and others, seems of the greatest interest to the problem of the house and the city.

[30] *Progressive Architecture*, XLVIII, No. 5 (May 1967), p. 144. There was also the real security of guards at the gate, but the symbolic aspect seems to have been more important—and probably even enters into the value of the guard.

*FIG. 6.1. Symbol of house—
the type of house drawn by London children
who were born and grew up in
multistory housing. (Adapted from Cowburn,
"Popular Housing," Arena, Sept.-Oct., 1966.)*

his own stakes into the ground, staking out his own little share of the land. No matter how small, he likes his own frontier to be distinct. In it he's safe and he's happy. That's what a fence is." [31] In the United States, fences have not been popular in the past, but there has lately been a considerable increase in fence sales which may well be due to an identification of fences with privacy—and privacy is becoming a status symbol.

In the same way, "roof" is a symbol of home, as in the phrase "a roof over one's head," and its importance has been stressed in a number of studies. In one study, the importance of images—i.e., symbols—for house form is stressed, and the pitched roof is said to be symbolic of shelter while the flat roof is not, and is therefore unacceptable on symbolic grounds.[32] Another study of this subject shows the importance of these aspects in the choice of house form in England, and also shows that the pitched, tile roof is a symbol of security. It is considered, and even shown in a building-society advertisement, as an umbrella, and the houses directly reflect this view.[33]

Another factor of the greatest importance is stress on the freestanding house in its own clearly defined plot of land facing an ordinary road, expressing anonymity and avoiding any form of grouping.[34] This, I think, explains the general nonacceptance of cluster housing. "What is sought for, and offered, is a symbol of an ideal life, varied in minor degree to suit differences in the individual interpretations or understanding of this ethos." [35] This is close to my "model and variations" interpretation of vernacular, and very different from the architect designed house and *its* values. The popular house is based on the ideal that one's home is indeed one's castle, and on a belief in independence. The house is to be as private and isolated as possible, with a moatlike separation; even children who have always lived in tall London apartment blocks draw houses in this way (Fig. 6.1).[36]

---

31 Quoted in Charles McCabe's column, "Please Fence Me In," *San Francisco Chronicle*, April 4, 1967. The important aspect of the fence is therefore symbolic rather than real. Compare Lawrence Halprin, *Cities* (New York: Reinhold Publishing Corporation, 1963), p. 37, where he points out that the garden in Japan is so small that it is "in a sense a series of symbols whose calligraphy is culturally understood through long accepted convention. The garden has become an abstraction of nature."
32 Cramer, "Images of Home," p. 42.
33 William Cowburn, "Popular Housing," *Arena: Journal of the Architectural Association* (London), September-October 1966, p. 81.
34 *Ibid.*, 76-77.
35 *Ibid.*, 77.
36 *Ibid.*, 80.

Conclusion

All of the preceding evidence seems to fit the schema which I have proposed rather closely. Our era is one of reduced physical constraints. We can do very much more than was possible in the past, and criticality is lower than ever.[37] The result is the problem of excessive choice, the difficulty of selecting or finding constraints which arose naturally in the past and which are necessary for the creation of meaningful house form. This great freedom of choice, and the fact that house form can now be the domain of fashion, suggests the general validity of the concept of criticality and the primacy of socio-cultural factors, and all that this implies for the understanding of house form, as well as its choice. However, we act as though criticality were high and close fit to physical "function" were essential. I have already commented on the unspecialized nature of vernacular buildings, and their consequent success over time. There may lie the great lesson of vernacular building for our own day—the value of constraints to establish generalized, "loose" frameworks where the interplay of the constant and changeable aspects of man can find expression.

[37] This can be clearly noted in the changing fashions in furniture and interior design in any history of the subject. It is clear that the difference between a Victorian living room and one in a Mies van der Rohe house is not due to changes in physical needs, but rather to changes in the image, the symbol, the fashion.

selected references

The number of books, monographs, and papers on various aspects of the house is very great. This selected bibliography is a step toward filling the need for a major bibliography on the subject. Sources in a number of languages have been included, since much of the work has been published in languages other than English.

BOOKS AND MONOGRAPHS

Background and general

ABRAMS, CHARLES, *Man's struggle for shelter in an urbanizing world*. Cambridge: MIT Press, 1965.

ALEXANDER, CHRISTOPHER, *Notes on the synthesis of form*. Cambridge: Harvard University Press, 1964.

ARDREY, ROBERT, *The territorial imperative*. New York: Atheneum Publishers, 1966.

ARENSBERG, C. M., and S. T. KIMBALL, *Culture and community*. New York: Harcourt, Brace and World, Inc., 1965.

Aspects de la maison dans le monde. Brussels: Centre International d'Etude Ethnographique de la Maison dans le Monde, n. d.

BENEDICT, RUTH, *Patterns of culture*. Boston: Houghton Mifflin Company, 1959.

BIRKET-SMITH, KAJ, *Primitive man and his ways*. New York: Mentor Books, Inc., 1962.

BOULDING, KENNETH, *The image*. Ann Arbor: University of Michigan Press, 1964.

BRAIDWOOD, R. J., *Prehistoric men* (5th ed.). Chicago: Natural History Museum, 1961.

———, and G. R. WILLEY, eds., *Courses toward urban life*, Viking Fund Publications in Anthropology, No. 32. Chicago: Aldine Co., 1962.

BREESE, GERALD, *Urbanization in newly developing countries*. Englewood Cliffs, N.J.: Prentice-Hall, Inc., 1966.

BREUIL, H., and R. LAWTIER, *Les hommes de la pierre ancienne*. Paris: Editions Payot, 1951.

BROSSE, J., et al., *100,000 years of daily life*. New York: Garden Press, 1961.

BRÜGER, W., *Einfürung in die Siedlungsgeographie*. Heidelberg: Quelle & Meyer, 1961.

BUNDGAARD, J. A., *Mnesicles.* Copenhagen: Gyldendal, 1957.

CHILDE, V. GORDON, *What happened in history.* Harmondsworth, Middlesex: Penguin Books, 1961.

CLARK, GRAHAME, *World prehistory.* Cambridge: Cambridge University Press, 1965.

DEFFONTAINES, PIERRE, *Géographie et religions* (9th ed.). Paris: Librairie Gallimard, 1948.

DOLFUSS, JEAN, *Les aspects de l'architecture populaire dans le monde.* Paris: Albert Morancé, 1954.

DUBOS, RENÉ, *Man adapting.* New Haven: Yale University Press, 1965.

DUHL, LEONARD, ed., *The urban condition.* New York: Basic Books, Inc., 1963.

ELIADE, MIRCEA, *Cosmos and history: the myth of the eternal return.* New York: Harper & Row, 1959.

————, *The sacred and the profane.* New York: Harper & Row, 1961.

FEBVRE, L., *La terre et l'évolution humaine.* Paris: La Renaissance du Livre, 1922.

FITZGERALD, C. P., *Barbarian beds.* London: Cresset Press, 1965.

FORDE, C. DARYLL, *Habitat, economy and society.* New York: E. P. Dutton and Co., 1963.

FRAZER, SIR JAMES G., *The golden bough* (Abridged ed.). New York: The Macmillan Company, 1927.

GIEDION, SIEGFRIED, *The eternal present:* Vol. 1—*The beginnings of art;* Vol. 2—*The beginnings of architecture.* New York: Pantheon Books, Inc., 1964.

GRILLO, PAUL J., *What is design?* Chicago: Paul Theobald, 1960.

GUTKIND, E. A., *Community and environment.* London: Watts & Co., Ltd., 1953.

————, *Our world from the air.* Garden City, N.Y.: Doubleday and Co., 1952.

HALL, EDWARD T., *The hidden dimension.* Garden City, N.Y.: Doubleday and Co., 1966.

————, *The silent language.* Greenwich, Conn.: Fawcett Publications, Inc., 1961.

HAMMOND, P. E., ed., *Sociologists at work.* New York: Basic Books, Inc., 1964.

HOLLAND, L. B., ed., *Who designs America?* Garden City, N.Y.: Doubleday and Co., 1966.

HUNTINGTON, ELLSWORTH, *Civilization and climate* (3rd ed.). New Haven: Yale University Press, 1924.

————, *The human habitat.* New York: W. W. Norton & Company, Inc., 1963.

JUNG, CARL, *Man and his symbols.* Garden City, N.Y.: Doubleday and Co., 1964.

KIRA, ALEXANDER, *The bathroom.* Ithaca, N.Y.: Cornell University Center for Housing and Environmental Studies Research Report No. 7, 1966.

KOUWENHOEVEN, JOHN A., *The beercan by the highway.* Garden City, N.Y.: Doubleday and Co., 1961.

————, *Made in America.* Garden City, N.Y.: Doubleday and Co., 1962.

LANGER, SUSANNE, *Feeling and form.* New York: Charles Scribner's Sons, 1953.

LEROI-GOURHAN, ANDRÉ, *L'homme et la matière.* Paris: Albin Michel, 1943-45.

————, *Milieu et technique.* Paris: Albin Michel, 1945.

LÉVI-STRAUSS, CLAUDE, *Structural anthropology.* New York and London: Basic Books, Inc., 1963.

LÉVY-BRUHL, L., *Primitive mentality,* trans. Lilian A. Clarke. Boston: Beacon Press, 1966.

LORENTZ, KONRAD, *King Solomon's ring.* New York: Thomas Y. Crowell Company, 1952.

————, *On aggression.* New York: Harcourt, Brace and World, Inc., 1963.

MACDONALD, DWIGHT, *Against the American grain.* New York: Random House, Inc., 1962.

MAGUIRE, PAUL, *From tree dwelling to new town.* London: Longmans, Green & Co. Ltd., 1962.

MAIR, LUCY, *Primitive government.* Harmondsworth, Middlesex: Penguin Books, 1962.

Maisons dans le monde. Paris: Librairie Larousse, n. d.

MEAD, MARGARET, *Continuities in cultural evolution.* New Haven: Yale University Press, 1966.

————, *Cultural patterns and technical change.* UNESCO, 1953.

MOHOLY-NAGY, SIBYL, *Native genius in anonymous architecture.* New York: Horizon Press, 1957.

MUMFORD, LEWIS, *Art and technics.* London: Oxford University Press, 1952.

———, *The city in history.* New York: Harcourt, Brace and World, Inc., 1961.

———, *Technics and civilization.* New York: Harcourt, Brace and World, Inc., 1934.

PIGGOTT, STUART, ed., *The dawn of civilization.* London: Thames and Hudson, 1961.

READ, SIR HERBERT, *The origins of form in art.* New York: Horizon Press, 1965.

REDFIELD, ROBERT, *The little community.* Chicago: University of Chicago Press, 1958.

———, *Peasant society and culture.* Chicago: University of Chicago Press, 1965.

———, *The primitive world and its transformations.* Ithaca, N.Y.: Cornell University Press, 1953.

RIPLEY, S. DILLON, ed., *Knowledge among men* (Smithsonian Institution Symposium). New York: Simon and Schuster, Inc., 1966.

RUDOFSKY, BERNARD, *Architecture without architects.* New York: Museum of Modern Art, 1964.

SAUER, CARL O., *Agricultural origins and dispersals.* New York: American Geographical Society, 1952.

SCHNEIDER, WOLF, *Babylon is everywhere—the city as man's fate.* New York: McGraw-Hill Book Company, 1963.

SCULLY, VINCENT, *The earth, the temple and the gods.* New Haven: Yale University Press, 1962.

SEGALL, M. H., D. T. CAMPBELL, and M. J. HERSKOWITZ, *The influence of culture on visual perception.* Indianapolis: Bobbs-Merrill Co., Inc., 1966.

SERVICE, E. R., *The hunters.* Englewood Cliffs, N.J.: Prentice-Hall, Inc., 1966.

———, *Profile of primitive societies.* New York: Harper & Row, 1958.

SHAPIRO, H. L., *Homes around the world.* New York: The American Museum of Natural History, Science Guide No. 124, 1947.

SJOBERG, GIDEON, *The preindustrial city—past and present.* New York: Free Press of Glencoe, 1960.

SOPHER, DAVID E., *Geography of religions.* Englewood Cliffs, N.J.: Prentice-Hall, Inc., 1967.

SORRE, MAX, *Les fondements de la géographie humaine* (esp. Vol. 3, *L'habitat*). Paris: Armand Colin, 1952.

SPENGLER, OSWALD, *The decline of the west.* New York: Alfred A. Knopf, Inc., 1957.

TAX, SOL, ed., *Anthropology today.* Chicago: University of Chicago Press, 1962.

THOMAS, W. M., ed., *Man's role in changing the face of the earth.* Chicago: University of Chicago Press, 1956.

VARAGNAC, A., *Civilization traditionelle et genre de vie.* Paris: Albin Michel, 1948.

WAGNER, PHILIP L., *The human use of the earth.* New York: Free Press of Glencoe, 1960.

WAGNER, PHILIP L., and M. W. MIKESELL, eds., *Readings in cultural geography.* Chicago: University of Chicago Press, 1962.

WASHBURN, S. L., *Social life of early man,* Viking Fund Publications in Anthropology, No. 31. Chicago: Aldine Co., 1961.

WEYER, EDWARD JR., *Primitive peoples today.* Garden City, N.Y.: Doubleday and Co., n. d.

WOLF, ERIC, *Peasants.* Englewood Cliffs, N.J.: Prentice-Hall, Inc., 1966.

ZELINSKY, WILBUR, *A prologue to population geography.* Englewood Cliffs, N.J.: Prentice-Hall, Inc., 1966.

Serials, bibliographies

BIASUTTI, R., *Le razze e popoli della terra* (4 vols.). Torino, 1959.

Department of Scientific and Industrial Research (England), *Overseas building notes* (originally Colonial Building Notes). These, over a period of years, investigate various problems of building in the tropics and in the developing countries, and refer to traditional solutions.

HODGE, F. W., *Handbook of American Indians.* Washington, D.C.: Bureau of American Ethnology, United States Government Printing Office, various volumes, 1910 ff.

MURDOCK, G. P., et al., *Human relations area files.* New Haven, Conn.: Yale University Press, various dates.

Smithsonian Institution Annual Reports. Washington, D.C.: United States Government Printing Office, various volumes, 1878 ff.

STEWARD, J. H., ed., *Handbook of South American Indians*. Washington, D.C.: Bureau of American Ethnology, United States Government Printing Office, various volumes, 1964 ff.

TAYLOR, C. R. N., *A Pacific bibliography*. Wellington: The Polynesian Society, 1951.

TOLSTOV, S. P., ed. *Narody mira* (Peoples of the world). Moscow: Soviet Academy of Sciences, 5 volumes from 1954-1959.

UNESCO, *History of Mankind* (cultural and scientific development), 2 volumes so far. Vol. 1, *Prehistory and the beginnings of civilization* (Jacquetta Hawkes and Sir Leonard Wooley); Vol. 2, *The ancient world* (Luigi Paretti et al.).

VON FISCHER-HEIMENDORF, E., *An anthropological bibliography of South Asia*. The Hague: Paer's, 1958.

WEST, R. C., and J. P. AUGELLI, *Middle America*. Englewood Cliffs, N.J.: Prentice-Hall, Inc., 1966.

Specific topics

ANDERSON, C. R., *Primitive shelter* (a study of structure and form in the earliest habitations of man). The Bulletin of Engineering and Architecture, No. 46. Lawrence, Kansas: University of Kansas, 1960.

ARONIN, J. E., *Climate and architecture*. New York: Reinhold Publishing Corporation, 1953.

DAVEY, NORMAN, *History of building materials*. London: Phoenix House, 1961.

HAUSER, HANS-OLE, *I built a stone age house*, trans. M. Michael. New York: John Day Company, Inc., 1964.

HONIES, FINN, *Wood in architecture*. New York: F. W. Dodge, 1961.

LEE, DOUGLAS H. K., *Physiological objectives in hot weather housing*. Washington, D.C.: HHFA, 1953.

LINDER, WERNER, *Bauwerk und Umgebung*. Tübingen: Verlag Ernst Wasmuth, 1964.

OLGYAY, VICTOR, *Design with climate*. Princeton: Princeton University Press, 1963.

PETERS, PAULHANS, *Atriumhäuser*. Munich: Callway, 1961.

RAGLAN, LORD, *The temple and the house*. New York: W. W. Norton & Company, Inc., 1964.

SCHOENAUER, N., and S. SEEMAN, *The court garden house*. Montreal: McGill University Press, 1962.

SHARP, THOMAS, *The anatomy of the village*. Harmondsworth, Middlesex: Penguin Books, 1946.

SINGER, CHARLES, et al., eds., *History of technology*. Oxford: Oxford University Press, 1954.

Specific areas—countries and regions. This group is particularly large, since most work is in the form of monographs on specific areas. There are also many travel books, descriptions, and local archives and histories which are useful.

Abert's New Mexico report, foreword by W. A. Keleher. Albuquerque: Horn and Wallace, 1962.

ALIZADE, G., *Narodnoye zodchestvo Azarbaidzhana i ego progressivniye traditsii* (The folk architecture of Azarbeidjan and its progressive traditions). Baku: Academy of Sciences, 1963.

ALNAES, EYVIND, et al., *Norwegian architecture through the ages*. Oslo: Aschehong and Co., 1950.

Architects' yearbook 10. London: Paul Elek, 1962 (paper by Pat Crooke).

Architects' yearbook 11. ("The pedestrian in the city"). London: Paul Elek, 1965 (papers by Herman Haan and Eleanor Smith Morris).

Architectura popular em Portugal (2 vols.). Lisbon: National Union of Architects, 1961.

ASCHEPKOV, E., *Russkoye narodnoye zodchestvo v Zapadnoi Sibiri* (Russian folk architecture of Western Siberia). Moscow: Soviet Academy of Architecture, 1950.

BALANDIER, GEORGES, *Afrique Ambiguë*. Paris: Librairie Plon, 1957. English translation by H. Weaver. New York: Pantheon Books, 1966.

————, and J-CL. PAUVERT, *Les villages gabonais* (Memoirs de l'Institut d'Études Centrafricaines No. 5). Brazzaville, 1952.

BALDACCI, OSVALDO, *La casa rurale en Sardegna.* Florence: Centro di Studii per la geograpia etnologica, 1952.

BARBIERI, GIUSEPPE, *La casa rurale nel Trentino.* Florence: L. S. Olschki, 1957.

BAUDIN, L., *Daily life in Peru under the last Incas.* London: Allen and Unwin Ltd., 1964.

BEGUIN, KALT, et al., *L'habitat au Cameroun.* Paris: Publication de L'office de la Recherche Scientifique Outre Mer & Editions de l'Union Française, 1952.

BEGUINOT, CORRADO, *Le valle del Sarno.* University of Naples, Institute of Architecture. Naples: Ed. Fausto-Florentino, 1962.

BENINCASA, E., *L'arte di habitare nel Mezzogiorno.* Rome: 1955.

BENNETT, W. C., and J. B. BIRD, *Andean culture history* (2nd ed.). Garden City, N.Y.: Doubleday and Co., 1964.

BIELINSKIS, F., et al., *Lietuvu liandes Menas* (Lithuanian folk art); includes 2 volumes on folk architecture. Vilnius: Government Publishing House, 1957-65.

BLASER, WERNER, *Classical dwellings in Japan.* Switzerland: Niggli Ltd., 1956.

BOETHIUS, AXEL, *The golden house of Nero.* Ann Arbor: University of Michigan Press, 1960.

BROCKMANN, HANS, *Bauern Haus im kreis Peine* (thesis at the Fakultät für Bauwesen). Hannover: Technische Hochschule, 1957.

BUNTING, BAINBRIDGE, *Houses of Boston's Back Bay* (An architectural history, 1840-1917). Cambridge: Belknap Press of Harvard University, 1967.

————, *Taos adobes.* Santa Fe: Museum of New Mexico Press, 1964.

BUSHNELL, G. H. S., *Peru.* New York: Frederick A. Praeger, 1963.

BUTI, G. G., *La casa degli Indeuropei.* Florence: Sansoni, 1962.

CARR RIDER, BERTHA, *Ancient Greek houses* (first published 1916). Chicago: Argonaut Inc., 1964.

CASTELLANO, M., *La valle dei Trulli.* Bari: Leonardo da Vinci, 1960.

CHAMBERLAIN, S., *Six New England villages.* New York: Hastings House, 1948.

CHEN, CHI-LU, *Houses and woodcarving of the Budai Rukai.* Reprint from the Bulletin of the Ethnological Society of China, Vol. VII, June 1958, Taipei, Taiwan, China.

COVARRUBIAS, MIGUEL, *The eagle, the jaguar and the serpent* (Indian arts of the Americas). New York: Alfred A. Knopf, Inc., 1954.

DJELEPY, PANOS, *L'architecture populaire en Grèce.* Paris: Albert Morancé, 1953.

DONAT, JOHN, ed., *World architecture 2.* London: Studio Books, 1965.

DOYON, GEORGES, and ROBERT HUBRECHT, *L'architecture rurale et bourgeoise en France.* Paris: Vincent Freal, 1945.

DRIVER, HAROLD E., *Indians of North America.* Chicago: University of Chicago Press, 1961.

DUGGAN-CRONIN, A. M., *The Bantu tribes of South Africa.* Cambridge: Deighton Bell, 1928.

DUPREY, K., *Old houses on Nantucket.* New York: Architectural Book Publishing Company, 1965.

ENGEL, HEINRICH, *The Japanese house.* Tokyo: Tuttle Co., 1964.

FLORIN, LAMBERT, *Ghost town treasures.* Seattle: Superior Publishing Co., 1965.

FONTYN, LADISLAV, *Volkbaukunst der Slowakei.* Prague: Artia, 1960.

GASPARINI, G., *La arquitectura colonial en Venezuela.* Caracas: Editiones Armitano, 1965.

GHEERBRANT, ALAIN, *Journey to the far Amazon.* New York: Simon and Schuster, 1954.

GHOSE, BENOY, *Primitive Indian architecture.* Calcutta: Firma K. L. Mukhopaday, 1953.

GIMBUTAS, J., *Das Dach des Litauischen Bauernhauses aus dem 19en. jahrhundert.* Stuttgart, 1948.

GOULD, MARY, *The early American house.* Rutland, Va.: Charles Tuttle, 1965.

GRABRIJAN, D., and J. NEIDHARDT, *Architecture of Bosnia.* Ljubljana: Državna Založba Slovenije, 1957.

GRANT, C., *The rock paintings of the Chumash* (A study of California Indian cultures). Berkeley and Los Angeles: University of California Press, 1965.

GREEN, M. M., *Ibo Village affairs.* New York: Frederick A. Praeger, 1964.

140

GRIFFEN, HELEN S., *Casas and courtyards—historic adobes of California*. Oakland, Calif.: Biobooks, 1955.

GUIART, JEAN, *Arts of the South Pacific*, trans. A. Christie. New York: Golden Press, 1963.

GUPPY, NICHOLAS, *Wai-Wai*. Harmondsworth, Middlesex: Penguin Books, 1961.

HAGEMANN, ELIZABETH, *Navaho trading days*. Albuquerque: University of New Mexico Press, 1963.

HANDY, E. S. C., and W. C. HANDY, *Samoan house building, cooking and tattooing*. Honolulu: Bishop Museum, 1924.

HART, D. V., *The Cebuan Filipino dwelling in Caticuyan*. New Haven: Yale University S.E. Asian Studies Center, 1959.

HENDERSON, A. S., *The family house in England*. London: Phoenix House, 1964.

HICKEY, GERALD C., *Village in Vietnam*. New Haven: Yale University Press, 1964.

HOOKER, MARION C., *Farmhouses and small buildings in Southern Italy*. New York: Architectural Book Publishing Co., 1925.

HOWETT, EDGAR L., *Pajarito plateau and its ancient people*. Albuquerque: University of New Mexico Press, 1953.

HUTCHINSON, R. W., *Prehistoric Crete*. Harmondsworth, Middlesex: Penguin Books, 1962.

ITOH, TEIJI, *The rural houses of Japan*. Tokyo: Bijuko-Shuppan, 1964.

KAWLI, GUTHORM, *Norwegian architecture past and present*. Oslo: Dreyers Verlag, and London: Batsford Ltd., 1958.

KEPES, G., ed., *Education of vision*. New York: George Braziller, 1965.

————, ed., *Sign, image, symbol*. New York: George Braziller, 1966.

KIDDER-SMITH, G. F., *Italy builds*. New York: Reinhold Publishing Corporation, 1955.

————, *Sweden builds* (2nd ed.). New York: Reinhold Publishing Corporation, 1957.

————, *Switzerland builds*. New York: A. Bonnier, 1950.

KOSOK, PAUL, *Life and water in ancient Peru*. New York: Long Island University Press, 1965.

KRUCKENHAUSER, S., *Heritage of beauty*. London: E. A. Watts, 1965.

KUBLER, GEORGE, *The art and architecture of Ancient America*. Harmondsworth, Middlesex: Penguin Books, 1960.

LA FARGE, OLIVER, *A pictorial history of the American Indian*. New York: Crown Publishers, 1956.

LAUBIN, R., and G. LAUBIN, *The Indian Tipi*. Norman: University of Oklahoma Press, 1957.

LÉVI-STRAUSS, CLAUDE, *Tristes tropiques*. Paris: Librairie Plon, 1955.

LEVIN, M. G., and L. P. POTAPOV, *Peoples of Siberia*. Chicago: University of Chicago Press, 1964 (this is part of the series *Narody Mira*).

LIU, TUN-CHEN, *A short history of the Chinese house*. Architectural and Engineering Publishing House, 1957. (This is an abridged translation by Mrs. Bryan and F. Skinner of a study done at Nanking.)

MCDERMOTT, J. F., ed., *The French in the Mississippi Valley*. Urbana: University of Illinois Press, 1965.

MAKOVETSKII, I. B., *Arkhitektura Russkogo narodnogo Zhilishcha* (The architecture of the Russian folk dwelling). Moscow: Soviet Academy of Science, Institute of Art History, 1962.

————, *Pamiatniki narodnogo Zodchestva srednego Povolzh'ia* (Monuments of folk architecture in the Central Volga region). Moscow: Academy of Science, 1952.

MARTIENSSEN, R. D., *The idea of space in Greek architecture*. Johannesburg: Wittwatersrand University Press, 1958.

MAUNIER, R., *La construction de la maison collective en Kabylie*. Paris: Institut d'Ethnologie, 1926.

MEGAS, GEORGE, *The Greek house*. Athens, 1951.

MEYER-HEISIG, E., *Die Deutsche Bauernstube*. Nürnberg: Verlag Karl Ulrich, 1952.

MINDELEFF, COSMOS, "A study of Pueblo architecture, Tusayan and Cibola," *Eighth Annual Report, Bureau of Ethnology*. Washington, D.C.: Smithsonian Institution, 1886-87; also studies in the same reports for 1894-95, 1897-98.

MOREHEAD, ALAN, *The blue Nile*. New York: Harper & Row, 1962.

————, *The white Nile.* New York: Harper & Row, 1961.

MORGAN, LEWIS H., *Houses and house life of the American aborigines* (1881). Republished Chicago: University of Chicago Press, 1965.

MORRISON, H. S., *Early American architecture.* New York: Oxford University Press, 1952.

MORSE, E. S., *Japanese homes and their surroundings* (first published 1886). New York: Dover Publications, Inc., 1961.

MOSSA, VICO, *Architettura domestica in Sardegna.* Cagliari: Ed. della Zattera, 1957.

MURDOCK, GEORGE P., *Africa, its people and their cultural history.* New York: McGraw-Hill Book Company, 1959.

NADER, LAURA, *Talea and Juquila* (A comparison of Zapotec cultural organization). Berkeley: University of California Publications in American Archeology and Ethnology, Vol. 48, No. 3, 1964.

NEWMAN, OSCAR, ed., *New frontiers in architecture.* New York: Universe Books, 1961.

NIGGLI, IDA, and H. MARDER, *Schweizer Bauernhäuser.* Tuefen: Verlag A. Niggli, n. d.

OLSEN, M., *Farms and fanes of ancient Norway.* Oslo: H. Aschehong Co., 1928.

OLSON, RONALD, *Adze, canoe and house types of the Northwest.* Seattle: University of Washington Publications in Anthropology, Vol. 2, 1927.

OPRESCU, GEORGE, *Peasant art in Rumania.* London: The Studio, 1929.

OVERDYKE, W. DARRELL, *Louisiana plantation homes.* New York: Architectural Book Publishing Co., 1965.

PAPAS, C., *L'Urbanisme et architecture populaire dans les Cyclades.* Paris: Editions Dunod, 1957.

PEASE, G. E., *The Cape of Good Hope 1652-1833.* Pretoria: J. L. Van Schaik, 1956.

PIRONNE, GIANNI, *Une tradition Européenne dans l'habitation* ("Aspects Européens" Council of Europe—Series A [Humanités No. 6]). Leiden: A. W. Sythoff, 1963.

PRICE, WILLARD, *The amazing Amazon.* New York: The John Day Company, 1952.

PRUSSIN, LA BELLE, *Villages in Northern Ghana.* New York: Universe Books, 1966.

RADIG, WERNER, *Frühformen der Hausentwicklung in Deutschland.* Berlin: Hanschel Verlag, 1958.

READ, KENNETH, *The high valley.* New York: Charles Scribner's Sons, 1965.

REDFIELD, ROBERT, *A village that chose progress: Chan Kom revisited.* Chicago: University of Chicago Press, 1950.

————, and A. VILLAROJAS, *Chan Kom: a Maya village.* Chicago: University of Chicago Press, 1934.

Rhodes-Livingstone Museum publications.

RUDENKO, S. I., ed., *Kazakhi* (The Kazakhs) (anthropological articles). Leningrad: Soviet Academy of Sciences, 1927.

SAMILOVITCH, B. P., *Narodna tvorchist' v arkhitekturi sil'skovo zhitla* (Folk creativity in rural dwelling architecture). Kiev: Institute of Architectural Study, 1961.

SANFORD, T. E., *The architecture of the Southwest.* New York: W. W. Norton & Company, Inc., 1950.

SEBASTIAN, LOPEZ S., *Arquitectura colonial en Popayan y Valle del Cauca.* Cali, Colombia, 1965.

Series on *Das Bürgerhaus* in different parts of Germany published by E. Wasmuth in Tübingen.

SHIBER, S. G., *The Kuwait urbanization* (no publisher or date).

SHIKIZE, K. I., *Narodnoe zodchestvo Estonii* (Folk architecture of Estonia). Leningrad, 1964.

SIMONCINI, G., *Architettura contadina de Puglia.* Genoa: Vitali and Ghianda, 1960.

SIS, V., J. SIS, and J. LISL, *Tibetan art.* London: Spring Books, 1958.

SMIALKOWSKI, RUDOLF, *Architektura i budownictwo pasterskie w Tatrach Polskich* (Architecture and construction of shepherd buildings in the Polish Tatras). Cracow: Government Scientific Publishing House, 1959.

SMITH, E. B., *Architectural Symbolism in Imperial Rome and the Middle Ages.* Princeton: Princeton University Press, 1956.

STANISLAWSKI, DAN, *The anatomy of eleven towns in Michoacan,* University of Texas Institute of Latin American Studies X. Austin: University of Texas Press, 1950.

STEINBRUECK, VICTOR, *Seattle cityscape.* Seattle: University of Washington Press, 1962.

STEPHEN, A. M., *Pueblo architecture,* Eighth annual report, Bureau of Ethnology, Smithsonian Institution. Washington, D.C., 1886-87.

STOIANOV, B. I., *Starata Rodopska arkhitektura* (The old architecture of the Rhodope, Bulgaria). Sofia, Techkniga, 1964.

STUBBS, STANLEY, *A bird's eye view of the Pueblos.* Norman: University of Oklahoma Press, 1950.

TAUT, BRUNO, *Houses and people of Japan.* Tokyo: Sanseido Co., 1958.

TAYLOR, A. C., *Patterns of English building.* London: Batsford, 1963.

THESIGER, WILFRED G., *The marsh Arabs.* New York: E. P. Dutton & Co., 1964.

TITZ, A. A., *Russkoe kamennoe zhiloe zodchestvo XVII veka* (Russian domestic stone architecture of the 17th century). Moscow: Soviet Academy of Sciences, 1966.

TRANTER, N., *The fortified house in Scotland.* London and Edinburgh: Oliver and Boyd, 1966.

TROWELL, M., *African design.* New York: Frederick A. Praeger, 1960.

———, and K. P. WACHSMAN, *Tribal crafts of Uganda.* Oxford: Oxford University Press, 1953.

UNDERHILL, R., *Indians of the Pacific Northwest.* Washington, D.C.: U.S. Department of the Interior, 1944.

VIDAL, F. S., *The oasis of Al-Hasa.* New York: Arabian-American Oil Co., 1955.

VON FÜRER-HEIMENDORF, C., *The Sherpas of Nepal.* Berkeley and Los Angeles: University of California Press, 1964.

WALTON, JAMES, *African villages.* Pretoria: J. L. Van Schaik, 1956.

———, *Homesteads and villages of South Africa.* Pretoria: J. L. Van Schaik, 1952.

WATERMAN, THOMAS T., and RUTH GRIME, *Indian houses of Puget Sound.* New York: Museum of the American Indian, 1921.

WATERMAN, THOMAS T., et al., *Native houses of Western North America.* New York: Museum of the American Indian, 1921.

WATSON, DON, *Cliff-dwellings of the Mesa Verde.* Mesa Verde National Park, Colorado, n. d.

WEISS, RICHARD, *Häuser und Landschaften der Schweiz.* Erlenbach (Switzerland): Eugen Rentsch Verlag, 1959.

WYCHERLEY, R. E., *How the Greeks built cities* (2nd ed). London: Macmillan & Co. Ltd., 1962.

ZASYPKIN, B. N., *Arkhitektura srednei Azii drevnich i srednich vekov* (Ancient and medieval architecture of Central Asia). Moscow: Soviet Academy of Architecture, 1948.

Selected studies on nondomestic vernacular building

ABRAHAM, R. J., *Elementare architektur.* Salzburg: Residentz Verlag, n. d.

ADAMS, K. A., *Covered bridges of the West.* Berkeley, California: Howell-North Books.

BRETT, LIONEL, *Landscape in distress.* London: The Architectural Press, 1965.

GREEN, E. R. R., *The industrial archeology of County Down.* Belfast: HMSO, 1963.

HUDSON, K., *Industrial archeology—an introduction.* Philadelphia: Dufour Editions, 1964.

KUBLER, GEORGE, *The religious architecture of New Mexico.* Colorado Springs, 1940 (republished 1962 by the Rio Grande Press).

MINER, HORACE, *The primitive city of Timbuctoo.* Garden City, N.Y.: Doubleday and Co., 1965.

MIRSKY, JEANETTE, *Houses of God.* New York: Viking Press, 1965.

Old European cities (16th century pictorial maps). London: Thames and Hudson, 1965.

PIECHOTKA, M., and K. PIECHOTKA, *Wooden synagogues.* Warsaw: Arkady, 1959.

RICHARDS, J. M., *The functional tradition.* London: The Architectural Press, 1958.

SCHMITT-POST, HANS, *Altkölnisches Bilderbuch.* Köln: Greven Verlag, 1960.

SLOANE, ERIC, *American barns and covered bridges.* New York: Wilfred Funk, 1954.

REFERENCES IN PERIODICALS

Articles on domestic architecture

ANDERSON, EDGAR, "The city is a garden," *Landscape*, VII, No. 2 (Winter 1957-58), 3-5.

ANDERSON, PETER, "Some notes on indigenous houses of the Pacific," *Tropical Building Studies*, University of Melbourne, II, No. 1 (1963).

A. W. C., "Village Types in the Southwest," *Landscape,* II, No. 1 (Spring 1952), 14-19.

BACHELARD, GASTON, "The house protects the dreamer," *Landscape,* XIII, No. 3 (Spring 1964), 28 ff.

BAINART, JULIAN, "The ability of the unprofessional: an African resource," *Arts and Architecture* (September 1966), pp. 12-15.

BALANDIER, GEORGES, "Problèmes économiques et problèmes politiques au niveau du Village Fang," *Bulletin d'Institut d'Etudes Centrafricaines,* Nouvelle séries No. 1, Brazzaville & Paris (1950), pp. 49-64.

"Bantu houses," *Architectural Design* (June 1962), p. 270.

BAWA, G., and U. PLESNER, "Traditional Ceylonese architecture," *Architectural Review* (February 1966), pp. 143-144.

BENNETT, ALBERT L., "Ethnographical notes on the Fang," *Journal of the Anthropological Institute* (London), XXIX, No. 1 (new series, vol. II), 1889, 66-98.

BINET, J., "L'habitation dans la subdivision de Foumbot," *Etudes Camerounaises,* III, No. 31-32 (September-December 1950), 189-199.

BOAS, FRANZ, "Houses of the Kwakiutl Indians," *Proceedings of the American Museum of Natural History,* XI (1888).

BRODRICK, A. H., "Grass roots," *Architectural Review* (February 1954), pp. 101-111.

BUSHNELL, DAVID, "Ojibwa habitations and other structures," *Smithsonian Institution Annual Reports,* 1917.

"Cappadocia," *Architectural Review* (April 1964), pp. 261-263.

"Cave dwellings of Cappadocia," *Architectural Review* (October 1958), pp. 237-240.

COCKBURN, CHARLES, "Fra-Fra house," *Architectural Design* (June 1962), pp. 299 ff.

COWBURN, WILLIAM, "Popular housing," *Arena: Journal of the AA* (London), September-October 1966.

CRANE, JACOB L., "Huts and houses in the tropics," *Unasylva* (United Nations Food and Agriculture Organization), III, No. 3 (June 1949).

CRESWELL, ROBERT, "Les concepts de la maison: les peuples non-industriels," *Zodiac,* VII (1960), 182-197.

DEMANGEON, A., "L'habitation rurale en France—essai de classification," *Annales de géographie,* XXIX, No. 161 (September 1920), 351-373.

"Djerba—an island near Tunis," *Architectural Review* (November 1965), pp. 273-274.

DODGE, STANLEY D., "House types in Africa," *Papers of the Michigan Academy of Science, Arts and Letters,* X (1929), 59-67.

EDALLO, AMOS, "Ruralism," *Landscape,* III, No. 1 (Summer 1953), 17 ff.

EHRENKRANTZ, EZRA D., "A plea for technical assistance to overdeveloped countries," *Ekistics* (September 1961), pp. 167-172.

ENGEL, DAVID, "The meaning of the Japanese garden," *Landscape,* VIII, No. 1 (Autumn 1958), 11-14.

FEILBERG, C. G., "Remarks on some Nigerian house types," *Folk* (Copenhagen), I (1959), 15-26.

FERDINAND, KLAUS, "The Baluchistan barrel vaulted tent and its affinities," *Folk* (Copenhagen), I (1959), 27-50.

FERREE, BARR, "Primitive architecture—sociological factors," *The American Naturalist,* XXIII (1889), 24-32.

FISCHER, OTTO, "Landscape as symbol," *Landscape,* IV, No. 3 (Spring 1955), 24-33.

FITCH, JAMES MARSTON, and DANIEL P. BRANCH, "Primitive architecture and climate," *Scientific American,* CCVII, No. 6 (December 1960), 134-144.

FOYLE, ARTHUR M., "Houses in Benin," *Nigeria,* No. 42 (1953), 132-139.

FUSON, ROBERT H., "House types of Central Panama," *Annals of the Association of American Geographers,* LIV, No. 2 (June 1964), 190-208.

GEBHART, DAVID, "The traditional wood houses of Turkey," *AIA Journal* (March 1963), pp. 36 ff.

GERMER, J. L., "Architecture in a nomadic society," *Utah Architect,* No. 39 (Fall 1965), 21-23.

GOLDFINGER, MYRON, "The Mediterranean town," *Arts and Architecture* (February 1966), pp. 16-21.

————, "The perforated wall," *Arts and Architecture* (October 1965), pp. 14-17.

GOTTMANN, JEAN, "Locale and architecture," *Landscape*, VII, No. 1 (Autumn 1957), 17-26.

GRANDIDIER, GUILLAUME, "Madagascar," *The Geographical Review* (New York), X, No. 4 (October 1920), 197-222.

GULICK, JOHN, "Images of the Arab city," *Journal of the AIP* (August 1963), pp. 179-197.

HICKS, JOHN T., "The architecture of the high Atlas Mountains," *Arena: Journal of the AA* (London), September-October 1966, pp. 85 ff.

HOPE, JOHN, "Living on a shelf" (a house at Lindos, Rhodes), *Architectural Review* (July 1965), pp. 65-68.

HORGAN, PAUL, "Place, form and prayer," *Landscape*, III, No. 2 (Winter 1953-54), 7-11.

HUBER, BENEDIKT, "Stromboli-architektur einer insel," *Werk*, XLV, No. 12 (December 1958), 428 ff.

ISAAC, ERICH, "The act and the covenant: the impact of religion on the environment," *Landscape*, XI, No. 2 (Winter 1961-62), 12-17.

———, "Myths, cults and livestock breeding," *Diogenes*, No. 41 (Spring 1963), 70-93.

———, "Religion, landscape and space," *Landscape*, IX, No. 2 (Winter 1959-60), 14-17.

JACK, W. MURRAY, "Old houses of Lagos," *Nigeria*, No. 46 (1955), 96-117.

JACKSON, J. B., "Chihuahua—as we might have been," *Landscape*, I, No. 1 (Spring 1951), 14-16.

———, "Essential architecture," *Landscape*, X, No. 3 (Spring 1961), 27-30.

———, "First comes the house," *Landscape*, II, No. 2 (Winter 1959-60), 26-35.

———, "The other directed house," *Landscape*, VI, No. 2 (Winter 1956-57), 29-35.

———, "Pueblo architecture and our own," *Landscape*, III, No. 2 (Winter 1953-54), 11 ff.

———, "The Westward moving house," *Landscape*, II, No. 3 (Spring 1953), 8-21.

LANNING, E. P., "Early man in Peru," *Scientific American*, CCXIII, No. 4 (October 1965), 68 ff.

"Ma'Aloula" (Syria), *Architectural Review* (October 1965), pp. 301-302.

MEYERSON, MARTIN, "National character and urban form," *Public Policy* (Harvard), XII (1963), 78-96.

MINER, HORACE, "Body ritual among the Nacirema," *American Anthropologist*, LVIII (1956), 503-507.

MOUGHTIN, J. C., "The traditional settlements of the Hausa people," *Town Planning Review* (April 1964), pp. 21-34.

PERRY, BRIAN, "Nigeria—design for resettlement," *Interbuild* (London) (January 1964), pp. 18-23.

PICKENS, BUFORD L., "Regional aspects of early Louisiana architecture," *Journal of the Society of Architectural Historians*, VII, No. 1-2 (January-June 1948), 33-36.

PIGGOTT, STUART, "Farmsteads in Central India," *Antiquity*, XIX, No. 75 (September 1945), 154-156.

POSENER, J., "House traditions in Malaya," *Architectural Review* (October 1961), pp. 280-283.

PRUSSIN, LA BELLE, "Indigenous architecture in Ghana," *Arts and Architecture* (December 1965), pp. 21-25.

PUSKAR, I., and I. THURZO, "Peasant architecture of Slovakia," *Architectural Review* (February 1967), pp. 151-153.

RAPOPORT, AMOS, "The architecture of Isphahan," *Landscape*, XIV, No. 2 (Winter 1964-65), 4-11.

———, "Yagua, or the Amazon dwelling," *Landscape*, XVI, No. 3 (Spring 1967), 27-30.

RUDOFSKY, BERNARD, "Troglodytes," *Horizon*, IX, No. 2 (1967).

SAINI, B. S., "An architect looks at New Guinea," *Architecture in Australia* (Journal of the RAIA), LIV, No. 1 (March 1965), 82-107.

SANDA, J., and M. WEATHERALL, "Czech village architecture," *Architectural Review*, CIX, No. 652 (April 1951), 255-261.

SANTIAGO, MICHEL, "Beyond the Atlas," *Architectural Review* (December 1953), pp. 272 ff.

"Santorini," *Architectural Review* (December 1958), pp. 389-391.

SKOLLE, J., "Adobe in Africa," *Landscape,* XII, No. 2 (Winter 1962-63), 15-17.

SOPHER, DAVID, "Landscapes and seasons: man and nature in India," *Landscape,* XIII, No. 3 (Spring 1964), 14-19.

SPENCE, B., and B. BIERMAN, "M'Pogga," *Architectural Review,* CXIV, No. 691 (July 1954), 35-40.

SPENCER, WILLIAM, "The Turkish village," *Landscape,* VII, No. 3 (Spring 1958), 23-26.

STEWART, N. R., "The mark of the pioneer," *Landscape,* XV, No. 1 (Autumn 1965), 26 ff.

THESIGER, WILFRED G., "Marsh Arabs," *Geographical Journal* (England), CXX (1954), 272-281.

———, "The marsh Arabs of Iraq," *The Geographical Magazine* (London), XXVII, No. 3 (July 1954), 138-144.

———, and G. O. Maxwell, "Marsh dwellers of Southern Iraq," *National Geographic Magazine,* CXIII, No. 2 (February 1958), 205-239.

THOMAS, ELIZABETH M., "The herdsmen," *The New Yorker* (May 1965), a series of four articles about the Dodoth.

"The troglodyte village of Gaudix, Spain," *Architectural Review* (March 1966), pp. 233 ff.

"Trulli," *Architectural Review* (December 1960), pp. 421-423.

TURNBULL, C. M., "The lesson of the Pygmies," *Scientific American,* CCVIII, No. 1 (January 1963), 28 ff.

VAN EYCK, ALDO, "Steps towards a configurative discipline," *Forum* (Holland), No. 3 (1962), 83 ff (this deals with the Pueblos).

VILLEMINT, ALAIN, "The Japanese house and its setting," *Landscape,* VIII, No. 1 (Autumn 1958), 15-20.

VON GRUENEBAUM, G. E., "The Muslim town," *Landscape,* I, No. 3 (Spring 1958), 1-4.

WATERMAN, THOMAS T., "Houses of the Alaskan Eskimo," *American Anthropologist,* XXVIII (1924), 289-292.

WATTS, MAY THEILGARD, "The trees and roofs of France," *Landscape,* X, No. 3 (Spring 1961), 9-14.

WEST, H. G., "The house is a compass," *Landscape,* I, No. 2 (Autumn 1951), 24-27.

WHEATLEY, PAUL, "What the greatness of a city is said to be" (review of Sjoberg's *The preindustrial city*), *Pacific Viewpoint,* IV, No. 2 (September 1963), 163-188.

WILLIAMS, DAVID, "Tukche—a Himalayan trading town," *Architectural Review* (April 1965), pp. 299-302.

WILMSEN, E. N., "The house of the Navaho," *Landscape,* X, No. 1 (Autumn 1960), 15-19.

WURSTER, WILLIAM W., "Indian vernacular architecture—Wai and Cochin," *Perspecta* (Yale Architectural Journal), No. 5 (1959), 37-48.

———, "Row house vernacular and high style monument," *Architectural Record* (August 1958), pp. 141 ff.

Some articles on nondomestic vernacular

"City mills, Perth, Scotland," *Architectural Review* (March 1966), p. 171.

"Greek mills in Iran," *Architectural Review* (April 1965), p. 311.

"Greek mills in Shetland," *Architectural Review* (July 1963), pp. 62-64.

MOUGHTIN, J. C., and W. H. LEARY, "Hausa mud mosques," *Architectural Review* (February 1965), pp. 155-158.

"Persian pigeon towers," *Architectural Review* (December 1962), p. 443.

RAPOPORT, AMOS, "A note on shopping lanes," *Landscape,* XIV, No. 3 (Spring 1965), 28.

———, "Sacred space in primitive and vernacular architecture," *Liturgical Arts,* XXXVI, No. 2 (February 1968), pp. 36-40.

———, and H. SANOFF, "Our unpretentious past," *AIA Journal* (November 1965), pp. 37-40.

index